Homemade
ON A
WEEKNIGHT

A FAMILY COOKBOOK
by Estelle Forrest

ISBN: 9798615823121
Imprint: Independently published

TABLE OF CONTENTS

Ethnic Adventures

Soups, Salads and Bowls

Healthier Fare

Side Dishes & Sauces

INTRODUCTION

When I set out on this adventure to write a cookbook, I did not realize what I was getting myself into. I have always loved to cook and loved to watch shows about cooking. I even enjoy reading cookbooks! In recent years I have found that cooking is my stress reliever — the kitchen has become my happy place. The more effort I put into my meals, and the more I experimented with different ingredients and techniques the more fun I was having. It is something to look forward to each day — which really helped me through some rough days. I also began to see the benefits of eating healthier as I started making things from scratch instead of from a jar/bottle/package. I got to a point where I was making a homemade meal every night for my family and loving it so much that I started posting photos of my plates on my social media. Then, my friends and family started asking for recipes and coming to me with questions and ideas about what to eat for dinner. As the interest grew, people started telling me I should write my own cookbook — so here we are!

WHO IS ESTELLE FORREST?

I am a lot of things — wife, mother, daughter, sister, niece, friend, business owner, volunteer, and a home chef. I have lived in the Pacific Northwest for most of my adult life and plan to stay forever — while traveling a lot. I am currently running a General Contracting business with my husband out of our home. Between us we have 6 kids in our blended family, 4 of which live with us full-time. We are a highly active family during the week — sports, bands, dance classes — as well as on the weekend — camping, hiking, car shows, and concerts. We like to go go go, but when it comes to dinnertime, we mostly like to dine-in! I love to create things with my hands and have probably tried almost every craft out there at least once or twice. Cooking is a huge part of my life. No matter what anyone says — you can taste the difference in the food if it was made with love. Some of the simplest meals can be elevated so much when they are cooked with care. Pouring love into the meals I create brings a feeling of fulfillment and satisfaction, not only to me, but to the people I care about.

WHAT DOES "HOMEMADE ON A WEEKNIGHT" MEAN?

For a lot of families, weeknights are so full of activities— sports, homework, housework, concerts, recitals, appointments, clubs, the list goes on. And we often feel like we must go to a drive-thru, eat some ready-made meal or a quick prep meal from a box. But it really is not true. Most of the reason we feel like we cannot cook homemade or "real" food on a weeknight is that we do not have the right set of tools in our arsenal. We need good, easy to follow recipes that have regular everyday ingredients. We need a few basic cooking techniques. And we need a plan. That is really all you need to start making homemade dinners every day of the week. Preparing a home cooked meal almost every day of the week is a sure way to get a true sense of accomplishment each day – you get to see your success on a plate!

This cookbook is going to be a little different for a few reasons. I have included plating directions on most recipes because I have learned over the years that children eat with their eyes first just like grown-ups and the best way to get them to try something new is to make it pretty! While I, personally, almost always use Organic ingredients, it does not mean you have to too, I make healthier versions of a lot of classic dishes but by no means is this cookbook a diet plan. It is about eating fresh-made dinners for a healthier lifestyle for the whole family. It is also about enjoying your food every day of the week, so the occasional indulgence is a must!

I have divided this cookbook in a way that I hope will make weekly meal planning easier. With 5 weeknights in mind, I have broken the recipes into 5 categories so that you can just pick one for each category for each day of the week. The Categories are Home Cookin', Ethnic Adventures, Healthier Fare, Soups, Salads, and Bowls, and Let's Get Fancy. With this sort of rotation, you have a solid 5 months of meal plans before having to repeat a meal. I promise - it will not get boring any time soon!

So, let's get cookin'!

Connect:

Facebook & Instagram: @HomemadeonaWeeknight

Web: homemadeonaweeknight.com

Email: homemadeonaweeknight@gmail.com

HOW TO READ THE RECIPES

Each recipe has some key components to make it easier to navigate. One very important step that I hope you will do with every single recipe is read it all the way through before starting to prepare it. This will help you ensure you have the right ingredients and tools readily available to you.

1. Every recipe instruction starts the same way – Prepare all of the ingredients. The reason for this is that having everything ready at the start of cooking is a huge stress reducer and a key to success. There is little worse than being in the middle of the recipe and realizing you have run out of paprika or that the bell peppers have gone bad or that prepping the cucumber takes longer than you thought it would. All of these things can really mess up your flow in the kitchen.

2. Many recipes will have plating notes at the bottom. As mentioned previously, plating your meals should be just as big a part as the ingredients themselves. We all eat with our eyes first and when something looks visually appealing it is just that much better. You will notice that a lot of the recipes call for a garnish of Parsley. This is a tried and true restaurant trick – it not only gives an appetizing contrast in color, but parsley actual enhances the flavors of any dish.

3. Some recipes have variations listed. This is to add to the versatility of the recipes. Many meals will work just as well with different proteins. If there are slightly different cooking times/techniques for the variation, I will list it.

4. To make the recipes for entire meals, you will find Side Dish Suggestions for recipes that are mostly just a main dish with a page number to easily find it.

5. Most recipes list the spices in a single line with the same measurements. This is not a misprint. I have found this to be one of the easiest ways to get even flavor throughout the recipe. Unless the instructions say otherwise, you can mix the seasonings as part of the prep stage and then add them all at once.

6. This cookbook does have a few photos of the recipes. If you would like to see photos of all the recipes, please visit the website – homemadonaweeknight.com and scroll through the recipe collections.

MEAL PLANNING

The idea of Meal Planning is not new, by any means. People, especially families, have been using some version of a meal plan for centuries. Depending on the size of your family, this could be a means to create two meals while cooking only once. It is also a best practice for cutting down on food waste.

Planning out your meals for the week – or even month – is a super effective way to ensure that you are cooking homemade meals frequently. When you plan the meals for the week/month ahead of time, you can make a grocery shopping list so that you only need to go to the store once for that week. Having the ingredients on hand is another way to make sure you stick to your "cooking at home" plan. Making a meal plan also helps you to get good variety in your meals – whether it be ingredients or styles of food – which is especially important when it comes to keeping your kids and maybe even your partner - interested in healthier meals.

This cookbook is designed to make meal planning super easy. The recipes are divided into 5 different categories and has the same number of recipes in each category so that you can literally pick one recipe from each category starting at the beginning and working your way down for 5 full months of 5 days a week meals before repeating a full meal. The side dishes at the end of the book as well as the recipe variations listed in some recipes will help you have some additional variety in your weekly meal planning by mixing and matching different recipes.

A few things to keep in mind for successful meal planning.

1. Choose a day each week for meal planning and then plan out the following weeks meals. At that time also make your grocery list so that you are ready to go. It is a good idea to take a snapshot of your menu each week, so that you can easily reference it at the store, or at the end of the day to remind yourself. Some people go as far as to enter it on their calendar, or in their planner.
2. Look at your calendar while come up with your plan so that you can think about how much time you have, or if some meal prepping needs to happen. For example, if you have an event that you need to attend that will limit the time for cooking and eating consider selecting a meal that has the same protein prepared in a similar way the previous night and preparing enough for both days. This might look like Chicken & Broccoli Alfredo (recipe pg. 37) one night followed by Chicken Salad Sandwiches (recipe pg. 95) on the busy night (since the chicken will be best cold in the second dish)

3. Always check what you have on hand when you are ready to make your weekly/monthly meal plan. One thing that deters people from home cooking is a fear of wasting fresh ingredients. If you stick to your plan you should not have this issue as often. To make the most of buying bulk – especially for meats – you want to make sure you are still using it in enough time.
4. If you will use the same protein two nights in a row, consider making sure that they are quite different styles of cooking. Quesadilla Explosion Salad (recipe pg. 76) followed by Creamy Red Enchiladas (recipe pg. 48) might not be a hit in your home but Chicken & Bacon Carbonara (recipes pg. 27) would be!

A WELL-STOCKED KITCHEN

Something that deters people from home cooking is not having all the ingredients on hand. When you must buy a whole bottle of a spice for one meal, it can increase the cost and make the whole concept seem overwhelming. While it is true that an initial kitchen set up can be daunting, it is simple. And if you purchase things that are used frequently in bulk, you typically can save some monies. It is always a good idea to read through all the recipes you have planned for the week, so that you do not find yourself mid-recipe with a missing ingredient.

Here are some items that will be helpful for success with the recipes in this cookbook.

1. Spices: Salt, Pepper, Parsley, Basil, Red Pepper Flakes, Oregano, Basil, Garlic Powder, Dill, Cumin and Onion Powder.
2. Dairy: Heavy Cream and Parmesan Cheese
3. Pantry Items: Variety of Pastas (Long & Short), Canned Crushed Tomatoes, Canned Tomato Sauce/Puree, Canned Black Beans, Canned Corn, Canned Refried Beans, Long Grain Rice, Coconut Milk, Flour, Avocado Oil, Apple Cider Vinegar and Chicken Broth.
4. Produce: Potatoes, Onion, Garlic
5. Meats: Chicken Breast, Frozen Shrimp, Variety of Sausages, Ground Turkey, Ground Beef, and Steak Filets.

Outside of the standard kitchen items – mixing bowls, pots, pans, cutting boards, knives, spoons, whisks, spatulas - some of the recipes call for some specific kitchen appliances/gadgets. But you do not necessarily need them all to create the meals. Here are some alternatives to specific gadgets.

1. Immersion Blender – a hand-held wand blender that making soups and veggies into creamy creations. For soups, you can use a regular blender. For veggies (potatoes and cauliflower) you can use a hand mixer or regular blender.
2. Griddle – a large flat cooking surface, either to be placed on top of stove burners or free-standing electric. You can always just use a frying pan; it will just have to be done in smaller batches.
3. Smoker – a wood-pellet burning grill. You can use a regular grill (charcoal or propane), it will just have a slightly different flavor. You can also use your oven if you have a cooking rack and a baking sheet.

HOME COOKIN'

Homemade on a Weeknight – Home Cooking

PARMA ROSA

Serves: 4-6   Prep Time: 10 min   Cook Time: 25 min

2 lb – Chicken Italian Sausage, cut in 1-inch chunks
2 28oz can - Crushed Tomatoes
1 15oz can- Tomato Puree
1 – Red Bell Pepper, cut into 1-inch pieces
1 small - Yellow Onion, diced
3 – Garlic Cloves, minced
1 cup – Parmesan, shredded
1 cup - Heavy Cream
1 tsp each: Basil, Oregano, Fennel Seed, Salt, Pepper, Red Pepper Flakes, Parsley
1 tbsp – Avocado Oil
1 ½ lb – Short Pasta (any variety)

1:
Prepare all of the ingredients. Start water boiling for pasta.
2:
In a large sauté pan over medium-high heat, add oil, onions, and garlic, and cook 3 minutes. Add the sausage and brown for 5 minutes, stirring occasionally. Last add the bell pepper and cook for 3 minutes then reduce heat to medium.
3:
Stir in the canned tomatoes and the seasonings. Let simmer for the rest of the time it takes the water to boil for the pasta. Put the pasta in the boiling water and cook as directed on the package.
4:
Add the heavy cream to the sauce and stir. Once totally incorporated, add the Parmesan cheese, a handful at a time.
5:
Drain pasta in a colander. Then rinse with cool water to arrest the cooking process.

Plating Notes: A portion of pasta in a shallow pasta bowl, ladle the sauce over and sprinkle with Parmesan cheese and parsley.

GARLIC & PARMESAN TURKEY MEATBALLS

Serves: 4-8   Prep Time: 10 min   Cook Time: 35 min

For the Meatballs:
2 lb - Ground Turkey
2 – Eggs, beaten
1/2 cup - Breadcrumbs
1/2 cup - Parmesan Cheese, shredded
3 – Garlic Cloves, minced
2 tbsp - Avocado Oil
1 tsp each: Salt, Pepper, Onion Powder, Parsley Flakes, Oregano, Basil

For the Sauce:
2 cups - Chicken Broth
2 cups - Heavy Whipping Cream
3 – Garlic Cloves, minced
2 cups - Parmesan Cheese, Shredded
1 tbsp- Corn Starch (mixed in 1/2 cup HOT water)
2 tbsp - Butter
1 tsp - Salt

1 ½ lb – Long Pasta (any variety)

1:
Prepare all of the ingredients. Start water boiling for pasta.
2:
In a large bowl, mix the ingredients for the Meatballs - minus the oil -
together. Hand roll the mixture into 1-inch meatballs. In a large sauté pan
over medium-high heat, add the oil. Place all of the meatballs into the pan,
cover and let cook for 5-7 minutes. Turn them each once and cover for
another 3-5 minutes. Remove the meatballs and set aside.
3:
In the same pan, add butter and garlic to the remaining oil. Let cook for 2
minutes. Then add the chicken broth and bring to a boil. Add salt. Whisk
in the heavy cream. Then add the corn starch/water mixture, continue
whisking until the sauce begins to thicken.
4:
Add the Parmesan cheese, 1/2 cup at a time, until fully mixed in. Reduce
the heat to medium and let it simmer about 10 minutes. Add the pasta to
the boiling water and cook as directed on the package. Return the
meatballs to sauce and let it warm through until the pasta is ready.

Plating Notes: Place a portion of the pasta in the center of a shallow bowl.
Place 4-6 meatballs atop the pasta, then ladle the sauce over the top.
Garnish with Parmesan Cheese and Parsley.

CHICKEN & SAUSAGE SKEWERS WITH BABY POTATOES

Serves: 4-6   Prep Time: 10 min   Cook Time: 35 min

For the Baby Potatoes:
2 lb - Baby Potatoes
2 tbsp – Avocado Oil
1 tsp each: Garlic Powder, Parsley, Salt, Black Pepper
8-10 Skewers

For the Chicken & Sausage Skewers:
1 ½ lb - Chicken thighs, boneless, skinless, cut into 1-inch cubes
2 1 lb - Chicken Sausage, cut into 1-inch slices
3 - Medium Green Bell Peppers, cut into 1-inch squares
4 2- Medium Red Bell Peppers, cut into 1-inch squares
1 – Medium Red Onion, cut into 1-inch squares
2 tbsp - Avocado Oil
1 tsp each: Garlic Powder, Parsley, Salt, Black Pepper
12-15 Skewers

1:
Prepare all of the ingredients. Preheat Grill or grill pan
to medium-high.
 2:
In a bowl, mix the potatoes with oil and seasoning until well
coated. Put 5-7 potatoes on each skewer. Make a foil packet
around the skewers and place the packet on the grill. Rotate them
every 10 minutes and allow to cook at least 25 minutes.
3:
In a bowl, mix chicken, sausage, bell peppers, oil and seasonings.
Make the skewers alternating meat and veggies. Place the
skewers directly on the grill. Rotate them every 5 minutes and
allow to cook for a total of 20 minutes.

Plating Notes: Each plate should get at least 1 potato skewer and
2 meat & veggie skewers. Either serve on the skewer or remove
the skewer as desired.

Side Dish Suggestion: Cucumber Salad (recipe pg. 118) or Corn
Salad (recipe. pg. 117)

WEEKNIGHT JAMBALAYA

Serves: 4-6   Prep Time: 5 min   Cook Time: 30 min

2 lb - Shrimp, peeled, deveined, tail-off
1 lb - Chicken Sausage, Andouille style, cut into 1-inch pieces
1 - 28oz can Crushed Tomatoes
1 qt – Chicken Broth
1 - Red Onion, Diced
4 – Garlic Cloves, minced
2 tbsp - Avocado Oil
2 - Bell Peppers, diced
1 – Buttered Rice (recipe pg. 124)
1 tsp each: Salt, Black Pepper, Basil, Oregano, Parsley
½ tsp – Cayenne Pepper

1:
Prepare all of the ingredients.
2:
In a large sauté pan over medium-high heat, add oil onions and garlic. Cook for 3 minutes. Next add sausage and brown for 8 minutes. Then add bell peppers and cook for 3 more minutes.
4:
Add chicken broth, seasonings, and crushed tomatoes. Cook for 5 minutes, then reduce heat to medium low. Simmer for 5 minutes then add shrimp. Put a lid on the pan and let it simmer for about 7 minutes.

Plating Notes: Put a portion of rice in a shallow bowl and ladle the yummy goodness of Jambalaya over the top. Garnish with parsley.

BEEF STROGANOFF

Serves: 4-6   Prep Time: 10 min   Cook Time: 30 min

1 ½ lb – Egg Noodles
1 ½ lb – Flank Steak, cut in ½-in pieces
2 cup – Baby Bella Mushrooms, sliced
½ - White Onion, sliced
2 tbsp – Avocado oil
2 – Garlic Cloves, minced
2 tbsp – Butter
2 tbsp – Flour (AP or Wheat)
2 cups – Beef Broth
1 cup – Heavy Cream
1 tsp each; Salt, Black Pepper, Parsley

1:
Prepare all of the ingredients. Start water boiling for noodles.
2:
In a large sauté pan over medium-high heat, add 1 tbsp oil, mushrooms, onions, and garlic. Cook for 6 minutes. Remove from pan and keep warm.
3:
In same pan, add remaining oil and steak pieces. Cook for 6 minutes then remove steak from pan and keep warm. Add noodles to boiling water and cook as directed on package.
4:
In the sauté pan, melt butter then add flour and seasonings and whisk together. Cook for 3 minutes. Whisk in broth and cook for 3 minutes then add heavy cream. Cook for 2 minutes then return the mushrooms and steak to pan. Cook for 3 more minutes.

Plating Notes: In a shallow bowl, place a portion of the egg noodles in the center than ladle steak, mushrooms, and gravy over top. Garnish with parsley, if desired.

OOEY GOOEY CHEESY CHICKEN & SPINACH ORZO

Serves: 4-6   Prep Time: 10 min   Cook Time: 20 min

2 lb - Chicken Thighs, boneless, skinless, cut into 1-inch cubes
1 ½ lb – Orzo Pasta
1 - Red Onion, diced
2 – Garlic Cloves, minced
2 tbsp – Avocado Oil
2 tbsp – Flour (AP or Whole Wheat)
1 tsp each: Thyme, Smoked Paprika, Parsley, Salt, Pepper
1 ½ cup - Sharp Cheddar, shredded
1 ½ cup - Chicken Broth
1 cup - Heavy Cream
1 cup - Baby Spinach, cut in ribbons (chiffonade)

1:
Prepare all of the ingredients. Start water boiling for pasta.
2:
In large sauté pan over medium-high heat, add oil, onions, and garlic. Cook for 3 minutes. Next add chicken cubes and seasonings. Stir occasionally, cook for 7 minutes.
3:
Add flour to the pan, mix thoroughly cook for 3 minutes. Add the chicken broth and fully incorporate.
4:
Put the orzo in boiling water and prepare as directed on the package. Add the heavy cream to the sauté pan slowly, while whisking. When the cream and broth are fully mixed, start adding the shredded cheese by the handful, mixing in each time.
5:
Strain the orzo and rinse with cool water to arrest the cooking process. Gently fold the orzo into the cheesy chicken sauce. Then fold in the baby spinach.

CHEESY HASH BROWN WAFFLES BREAKFAST PLATE

Serves: 6   Prep Time: 10 min   Cook Time: 30 min

4 cups – Russet Potatoes, shredded
1 cup - Sharp Cheddar Cheese, shredded
1 tsp each: Salt, Pepper, Onion Powder, Garlic Powder, Paprika
1 tbsp - Avocado Oil
12 - Eggs
6 - English Muffins
¼ cup - Butter
2 lb – Ham, thick-cut slices
1 lb - Mixed Fruit, cut

1:
Prepare all of the ingredients. Preheat oven to 450deg. Set waffle maker to High.
2:
In a mixing bowl combine potatoes, cheese, and seasoning.
3:
Start making waffles with 3/4 cup of hash brown mixture for each waffle. Continue with remaining waffle mixture.
4:
In a frying pan over medium-high heat, fry ham until just toasted and remove from pan.
5:
Fork split English muffins and place face up on a large baking sheet. Place a pat of butter on each muffin. Place in oven for 8 minutes.
6:
In a frying pan over medium-high heat, add oil. Fry eggs as desired, over medium is suggested. Salt and pepper as desired.

Plating Notes: Place one waffle, two eggs, two slices of ham and an English muffin (two sides) on a plate. Garnish plate with parsley. Serve fresh mixed fruit in a small bowl on the side.

Variation: Use a 30oz bag of frozen hash browns to speed up the process.

CHICKEN BACON RANCH CASSEROLE

Serves: 4-6   Prep Time: 15 min   Cook Time: 40 min

2 lb – Chicken Breast, cut into 1-inch cubes
1 lb – Red Potatoes, cut into 1-inch cubes
1 lb – Bacon, cut into ½-inch pieces
2 cup – Sharp Cheddar Cheese, shredded
2 tsp each: Salt, Pepper, Paprika, Ranch Seasoning, Garlic Powder
6 – Scallions, sliced
2 tbsp – Avocado Oil
½ cup – Sour Cream, for topping

1:
Prep all of the ingredients. Preheat oven to 400deg.
2:
In a frying pan over medium-high heat, add bacon. Cook until crispy and remove to paper towel covered plate.
3:
In a 13x9 baking dish, combine chicken, potatoes, seasoning, oil, half of the bacon and half of the scallions. Top with cheese and remaining bacon. Put in oven for 40 minutes.
4:
Allow to cool at least 5 minutes before serving.

Plating Notes: On a plate, spoon a portion of the casserole onto plate. Top with dollop of sour cream and scallions.

CHEESE & SPINACH STUFFED MEATLOAF

Serves: 4-6   Prep Time: 10 min   Cook time: 30 min

1 lb - Ground Beef
1 lb - Ground Pork
2 – Eggs, beaten
½ - White Onion, chopped
2 – Garlic Cloves, minced
1 tsp each: Salt, Pepper, Parsley, Smoked Paprika, Dill
1 cup - Sharp Cheddar, shredded
1 cup - Fresh Spinach

1:
Prepare all of the ingredients. Preheat oven to 375deg.
2:
In a large bowl, mix everything except the cheese and spinach.
Gently press half the mixture into a loaf pan. Layer with half the
shredded cheese, then the spinach, and the rest of the shredded
cheese. Lastly put the remaining meatloaf mixture on top and
press down the sides along the border to enclose the cheese and
spinach.
3:
Put the pan into a preheated 375F oven for 30 minutes. Let cool
for at least 10 minutes.

Side Dish Suggestion: Potatoes Au Gratin (recipe pg. 115) or Honey
Roasted Carrots (recipe pg. 127)

CHEESY CHICKEN SAUSAGE PASTA

Serves 4-6   Prep Time: 10 min   Cook time: 30 min

1 ½ lb – Chicken Sausage, cut into 1-inch chunks
1 tbsp – Avocado Oil
½ - White Onion, diced
2 – Garlic Cloves, minced
1 15oz can – Diced Tomatoes
2 cup – Chicken Broth
1 cup – Heavy Cream
1 lb – Short Pasta (Rotini or Penne)
2 cup – Sharp Cheddar Cheese, Shredded
1 tsp each: Salt, Red Pepper Flakes, Basil, Parsley

1:
Prep all of the ingredients.
2:
In a large pot over medium-high heat, add oil, onions, and garlic
and cook for 4 minutes. Next add sausage and cook for 4 minutes.
Add chicken broth, seasoning and tomatoes and bring a boil.
3:
Reduce heat to medium and add the pasta, cover, and cook for 15
minutes. Remove from heat and stir in heavy cream and cheese
until fully incorporated.

SHEET PAN STEAK DINNER

Serves: 4-6   Prep Time: 10 min   Cook Time: 25 min

2 tbsp – Avocado Oil, divided
2 lb – Flank Steak
1lb – Asparagus, ends cut
2 tbsp - Butter
1 – Garlic Clove, minced
1 tsp each: Salt, Pepper, Smoked Paprika, Garlic Powder, Rosemary

1:
Prepare all of the ingredients. Preheat oven to 400deg.
2:
On a large parchment paper covered baking sheet, add flank steak on one side and asparagus on the other. Brush both sides of flank steak with oil and seasoning mix.
3:
Melt butter and stir in fresh garlic. Pour butter mix over asparagus. Cover sheet pan with foil and add to top rack of oven for 25 minutes. Let steak rest for at least 5 minutes before slicing on the diagonal.

Side Dish Suggestion: Roasted Potatoes & Cauliflower (recipe pg. 120)

CHICKEN BACON RANCH WRAPS

Serves: 6   Prep time: 15 min   Cook time: 25 min

1 lb – Bacon, ½-inch pieces
6 – Tortillas, burrito size
1 cup – Ranch Dressing
6 pieces – Green Leaf Lettuce
1 – Tomato, thin sliced
1 cup – Cream Cheese, softened
1 cup – Cheddar Cheese, shredded

For the Chicken:
1 ½ lb - Chicken Breast, thin-sliced
1 cup – Flour (Whole Wheat or AP)
1 tsp each: Salt, Pepper, Paprika, Garlic Powder, Parsley
3 tbsp – Avocado Oil
2 – Eggs, beaten

1:
Prepare all of the ingredients.
2:
Make a dredging station: On first plate mix eggs, salt, and pepper.
On second plate, mix the flour and remaining seasonings. Then
dredge the chicken in the egg, then the flour. Repeat with all
pieces.
3:
In a large sauté pan over medium-high heat, add the oil. Cook
each breaded chicken for 7 minutes on each side. Set aside to
cool.
4:
In same large sauté pan over medium-high heat, fry bacon until
crispy. Remove to paper towel covered plate.
5:
On a tortilla, place a small amount of cream cheese in the center
as well as on one outer edge. Place a piece of lettuce, 2-3 pieces
of bacon, 2-3 slices of tomato, shredded cheese, and then
chicken. Drizzle with ranch dressing. Fold the sides of the tortilla
to the center than roll up and use the cream cheese on the edge
to hold it closed. Cut, on the diagonal, in the center and serve.

Side Dish Suggestion: Street Corn (recipe pg. 121) or Pasta Salad
(recipes pg. 126)

BACON & EGG QUICHE

Serves: 4-6   Prep Time: 10 min   Cook time: 35 min

15 – Eggs, beaten
1lb- Bacon, cut into ½-inch pieces
2 cups - Cheddar Cheese, shredded
1 tbsp - Parsley
1 tsp each: Salt, Pepper, Garlic Powder, Onion Powder

1:
Prepare all of the ingredients. Preheat oven to 400deg
2:
In a frying pan over medium-high heat, add bacon and cook until crispy. Drain on paper towel and let cool.
3:
In a large mixing bowl, beat together eggs and seasoning thoroughly. Then add cheese and bacon.
4:
Divide into 2 oiled 8-in pie pans. Put on top rack of oven for 30 minutes. Let cool 5 minutes before serving.

Variations: Use Sausage Links, cut into ½-inch pieces, or a variety of vegetables (mushrooms, broccoli, bell peppers, spinach, etc.)

BAKED MACARONI AND CHEESE WITH SAUSAGE

Serves: 4-6   Prep time: 10 min   Cook time: 35 min

1 lb – Chicken Sausage, Andouille Flavor, cut into 1-inch chunks
1 lb – Elbow or Shell Pasta
3 tbsp – Butter
3 tbsp – Flour (AP or Whole Wheat)
2 cups – Chicken Broth
1 cup – Heavy Cream
2 cups – Cheddar Cheese, shredded, divided
1 ½ cups – Parmesan Cheese, shredded, divided
1 tsp each: Garlic Salt, Pepper, Parsley, Paprika
1 lb – Bacon, cut into ½-inch pieces.

1:
Prepare all of the ingredients. Preheat oven to 425deg. Start water boiling for pasta.
2:
In a saucepan over medium heat, melt butter and add garlic salt and pepper. Whisk in flour and let cook for 3 minutes. Whisk in chicken broth and cook for 2 minutes. Whisk in Heavy Cream and cook 2 minutes. Whisk in 1 ½ cup Cheddar and 1 cup Parmesan Cheese and cook 2 minutes.
3:
Add the pasta to the boiling water and cook for 2 minutes less than directed on package. Drain and rinse with cold water to arrest the cooking process.
4·
In a frying pan over medium-high heat, add bacon and cook until crispy. Drain on paper towel.
5:
In a 13x9 baking dish, fill with cooked pasta and sliced sausage chunks. Pour cheese sauce over top and stir together to evenly coat. Top with remaining cheese and parsley. Place in oven for 25 minutes.
6:
Remove from oven and immediately sprinkle with bacon.

Variations: Replace sausage with Ham chunks.

JALAPENO POPPER CHICKEN

Serves: 6   Prep Time: 15 min   Cook Time: 30 min

6 – Chicken Breasts
8oz – Cream Cheese
½ cup – Sharp Cheddar Cheese, shredded
1 – Fresh Jalapeno, diced
1 tsp each: Salt, Pepper, Garlic Powder, Parsley
1 tbsp – Avocado Oil

1:
Prepare all of the ingredients. Preheat grill or grill pan
to medium-high
2:
In a mixing bowl, combine cheeses, jalapenos, and seasonings.
Place a chicken breast between two pieces of plastic wrap and
flatten to ½-inch thickness. Mound cream cheese mixture on one
half of chicken and fold chicken over, securing with toothpick.
Repeat with remaining chicken breasts. Brush outside of chicken
with oil.
3:
Place a large piece of foil on grill and place chicken breasts to cook
for 30 minutes, flipping once while cooking.

Side Dish Suggestion: Potato Salad (recipe pg. 125) or Corn Salad
(recipe pg. 117)

CHEDDAR FRIED CHICKEN

Serves: 4-6   Prep Time: 15 min   Cook Time: 30 min

1 ½ lb – Chicken Breast
3 cups – Cheddar Cheese, shredded
½ cup – Flour (AP or Wheat)
2 – Eggs, beaten
1 cup – Breadcrumbs
1 tsp each: Salt, Pepper, Garlic Powder, Paprika, Parsley
2 tbsp – Avocado Oil

1:
Prepare all of the ingredients.
2:
Place chicken between plastic wrap and pound out until 1/2in thick, then cut in half, crosswise. Repeat with each piece.
3:
Make a dredging station: On first plate, mix the eggs and seasonings. On second plate, mix the flour and cheese. On third plate, add the breadcrumbs. With each piece of chicken coat with the egg mix, then cheese mix, then breadcrumbs.
4:
In a large frying pan over medium-high heat, add 1 tbsp oil. Place several pieces of chicken in and cook for 5 minutes on each side, then remove to a plate with a paper towel over it. Add remaining oil to pan and cook remaining chicken.

Side Dish Suggestion. Pasta Salad (recipe pg 126) or Baked Cauliflower (recipe pg. 122)

Variations: For a buttery flavor, use crumbled Ritz Crackers instead of breadcrumbs. For slightly healthier version, use crumbled unsalted saltines.

ONE POT SAUSAGE & PEPPERS PASTA

Serves: 4-6   Prep Time: 10 min   Cook Time: 30 min

1 ½ lb – Sausage, cut into 1-inch pieces
1 tbsp – Avocado Oil
1 – Green Bell Pepper, cut into 1-inch pieces
2 1 – Red Bell Pepper, cut into 1-inch pieces
3 – Garlic Cloves, minced
1 lb – Short Pasta (rotini, farfalle, penne)
2 qt – Chicken Broth
1 cup - Heavy Cream
2 cup – Cheddar Cheese, shredded
1 tsp each: Salt, Pepper, Parsley

1:
Prepare all the ingredients.
2:
In a large pot over medium-high heat, add oil, sausage, and garlic. Let cook for 2 minutes, then add bell peppers. Let cook for 3 minutes, then add pasta and broth. Reduce heat to medium and cover pan. Cook for 20 minutes. Do not remove lid or stir during cook time.
3:
At the end of the cook time, stir in heavy cream, cheese, and seasonings. Let cook for 5 minutes, stirring occasionally.

Variations: Use Chicken Breast instead of Sausage. Prepare in same way but let chicken cook with garlic until no longer pink.

STUFFED MEATBALL PASTA

Serves: 4-6   Prep time: 15 min   Cook Time: 30 min

1 ½ lb — Spaghetti Noodles

For Meatballs:
1 lb — Ground Beef
1 lb — Ground Italian Sausage
2 — Eggs, beaten
2 — Garlic Cloves, minced
½ cup — Breadcrumbs
3 — Mozzarella String Cheese Sticks, cut into ¾-inch pieces
1 tsp each: Salt, Pepper, Oregano, Fennel Seed, Basil, Red Pepper Flakes

For Sauce:
2 28oz cans - Crushed Tomatoes
1 15 oz can - Tomato Sauce
½ - Onion, diced
3 - Garlic Cloves, minced
2 tbsp - Avocado Oil
1 tsp each: Salt, Pepper, Red Pepper Flakes, Basil, Oregano, Fennel, Parsley

1:
Prepare all of the ingredients. Preheat oven to 400deg. Start water boiling for pasta.
2:
In a large mixing bowl, combine all meatball ingredients except cheese chunks. Wrap meat mixture around a piece of cheese to make 1 ½ -inch balls. Place on greased cooking sheet. Put in oven and cook for 25 minutes.
3:
In a large sauté pan over medium-high heat, add oil, onions, and garlic. Cook for 4 minutes. Add crushed tomatoes, tomato sauce and sauce seasoning. Mix and lower to medium low and let simmer.
4:
Add pasta to boiling water and prepare as directed on the package.
5:
Remove meatballs from cooking sheet and add to sauce. Let cook for 5 minutes.

Plating Notes: On a plate or shallow bowl, place a portion of pasta in center. Ladle 4-6 meatballs onto center of pasta. Then ladle additional sauce over the top. Garnish with parmesan cheese and parsley if desired.

Variations: Use Ground Turkey instead of Ground Beef and add 1 tbsp of avocado oil with eggs to meatball mixture.

CHEDDAR BACON PORK CHOPS

Serves: 6   Prep Time: 10 min   Cook Time: 30 min

6 – Pork Chops, boneless
2 cups – Sharp Cheddar, shredded
1 lb – Bacon, cut in ½-inch pieces
3 – Scallions, sliced
1 tsp each: Salt, Pepper, Garlic Powder, Parsley

1:
Prepare all of the ingredients. Preheat oven to 400 deg.
2:
In a large sauté pan over medium-high heat, add bacon. Fry until crispy and remove to a paper towel covered plate. Remove all but 1 tbsp of bacon grease from pan.
3:
After sprinkling pork with seasonings, add to same pan and cook on each side for 5 minutes. Then place pork in 13x9 baking dish. Cover with shredded cheese, bacon bits and scallions. Put in oven for 20 minutes.

Side Dish Suggestion: Whipped Garlic Cauliflower (recipes pg. 112) or Honey Roasted Carrots (recipe pg. 127)

BACON & BLEU STEAK STUFFED POTATOES

Serves: 6   Prep Time: 10 min   Cook Time: 60 min

6 – Large Russet Potatoes
1 tsp – Salt

For Steak:
1 ½ lb – Flank Steak
1 tsp each: Salt, Pepper, Garlic Powder, Paprika 1 tbsp – Avocado Oil

For Filling:
8 oz – Bleu Cheese Crumbles
8 oz – Sour Cream
1 lb – Bacon, cut in ½-inch pieces
2 – Scallions, sliced

1:
Prepare the ingredients. Preheat oven to 400deg. Preheat grill or grill pan to medium-high heat.
2:
Arrange potatoes on baking sheet and sprinkle with salt. Place in oven for 45 minutes.
3:
Sprinkle steak with steak seasonings, then brush with oil. Place on grill and cook for 10 minutes on each side. Remove from grill and let rest for 10 minutes before cutting into bite-size pieces
4:
In a frying pan over medium-high heat, cook bacon until crispy. Remove to paper towel to drain excess oil.
5:
Remove potatoes from oven. Cut the top cap off of the potato and use a spoon to scoop out most of potato from the skin into a large mixing bowl. Place skins on baking sheet. Add cheese, steak, bacon, sour cream, and scallions to the cooked potatoes and gently combine. Evenly divide the mixture into the potato skins. Return the potatoes to oven for 10 additional minutes.

Variations: For a slightly healthier version of this, use Sweet Potatoes instead of Russet.

Side Dish Suggestion: Corn Salad (recipe pg. 117)

LET'S GET FANCY

INDIVIDUAL BEEF WELLINGTON

Serves: 1   Prep Time: 20 min   Cook Time: Varies (see below)

6 oz - Beef Tenderloin Steak
1 - Puff Pastry Sheet
5-7 - Baby Bella Mushrooms, minced finely
4 tbsp - Avocado Oil
1 tsp - Cooking Sherry
1 tsp each: Garlic Powder, Onion Powder, Thyme
2 tsp each: Salt, Pepper.

1:
Prepare all of the ingredients. Preheat your oven to 400deg.
2:
In a sauté pan over medium-high heat, add 2 tablespoons of oil, mushrooms, cooking sherry, garlic powder, onion powder, thyme, 1 teaspoon salt, and 1 teaspoon pepper. Continue to cook for 8 minutes and remove from pan.
3:
Salt and pepper steak. Add the remaining oil to pan. Sear all four sides of the steak and remove from heat.
4:
Lay out the sheet of puff pastry and use a rolling pin to flatten some. Put half of mushroom mixture in the center of the puff pastry. Place seared steak on top of the mushroom mix. Then put remaining mushroom mix on top of steak. Fold the puff pastry over the top of the steak to create an envelope. Pinch the edges together and cut off the excess .
5:
Using a cooking rack on a baking sheet, place the Wellington in the center of the sheet, and put it in the center of oven.
Cooking times:
Rare - 10-12 minutes
Medium Rare - 12-14 minutes
Medium - 14-16 minutes
Medium Well - 16-18 minutes
Well - 18+ Minutes
6:
Let Wellington sit for at least 5 minutes, on the rack before cutting into it.

Plating Notes: It is always best to serve a wellington sliced down the middle.

Side Dish Suggestion: Potato Stacks (recipe pg. 114)

BEEF & SAUSAGE STUFFED MUSHROOMS

Serves: 6   Prep Time: 10 min   Cook Time: 30min

1 lb - Ground Beef
1 lb Ground Pork Sausage
8 - Portabella Mushroom
2 - Eggs
2 tbsp – Avocado Oil
2 - Garlic Cloves, minced
1 - Small Red Onion, diced
1 tbsp - Parsley
1 tsp each: Salt, Black Pepper, and Smoked Paprika
1 cup - Mozzarella Cheese, shredded

1:
Prepare all of the ingredients. Preheat oven to 350deg.
2:
Remove stems and ribs from the mushroom caps. Place top down on a baking sheet and drizzle with oil.
3:
In a large mixing bowl, combine ground beef, ground pork, parsley, garlic, onion, egg, and ½ cup of mozzarella.
4:
Pack the meat mixture evenly into the caps. Top with the remaining mozzarella cheese. Place on a baking sheet. Put into oven for 30 minutes.

Side Dish Suggestions: Whipped Garlic Cauliflower (recipe pg. 112) or Pasta in Red Sauce (recipe pg. 128)

STUFFED SHELLS

Serves: 4-6   Prep time: 10 min   Cook Time: 30
min

1 box Jumbo Shells

For the sauce:
1 lb – Ground Italian Pork Sausage
2 28oz cans - Crushed Tomatoes
1 15oz can - Tomato Sauce
½ - Onion, diced
3 - Garlic Cloves, minced
2 tbsp - Avocado Oil
1 tsp each: Salt, Pepper, Red Pepper Flakes, Basil, Oregano,
Fennel, Parsley

For the filling:
1 32oz tub - Ricotta Cheese
1 – Egg, beaten
1 cup – Mozzarella Cheese, shredded
1 cup – Parmesan Cheese, shredded
1 tsp each: Parsley, Garlic Powder, Basil, Oregano

1:
Prepare all of the ingredients. Preheat oven to 400deg. Start
water boiling for pasta.
2:
Cook the shells just before al dente. Drain and rinse with cold
water. Set aside
3:
In a large sauté pan over medium-high heat, add oil, onions, and
garlic. Cook for 4 minutes. Add sausage and cook 4 minutes. Add
crushed tomatoes, tomato sauce and sauce seasoning. Mix and
lower to medium low and let simmer.
4:
Mix filling ingredients together thoroughly.
5:
In a 13x9 glass dish, put 1 inch of sauce in bottom. Fill each shell
with filling mixture and set in glass dish. Top with additional
sauce. Bake for 20minutes.

Plating Notes: On a plate or in a shallow bowl, ladle a small
amount of sauce onto the plate. Then place 4-6 shells in the
sauce. Garnish with parmesan cheese and parsley, if desired.

Variations: Use ground turkey instead of pork sausage or no meat
for vegetarian option.

CHICKEN & BACON CARBONARA

Serves: 4-6   Prep Time: 10 min   Cook Time: 25 min

1 ½ lb – Chicken Breast, cut into 1-inch pieces
2 – Garlic Cloves, minced
1 ½ lb – Spaghetti Noodles
1 lb – Bacon, ½-in pieces
1 cup – Parmesan Cheese, shredded
1 cup – Heavy Cream
1 tsp each: Salt, Pepper, Oregano, Basil, Parsley

1:
Prep all of the ingredients. Start water boiling for pasta.
2:
In a large sauté pan over medium-high heat, add oil and garlic, and cook 3 minutes. Then add chicken and seasoning and cook for 7 minutes.
3;
Add pasta to boiling water and cook as directed by the package.
4:
In a frying pan over medium-high heat, add bacon and cook until crispy. Drain on paper towel and let cool.
5:
Drain pasta and rinse with cool water. Add pasta to sauté pan. Stir in bacon, heavy cream, and parmesan cheese. Reduce heat to medium-low and let cook for 5 minutes.

PORK SCALLOPINI OVER CREAMY PASTA

Serves: 4-6   Prep Time: 10 min   Cook time: 25 min

1 ½ lb – Short Pasta (any variety)

For the Pork:
1 ½ lb - Pork Loin Filets, boneless
1 cup – Flour (Whole Wheat or AP)
1 tsp each: Salt, Pepper, Paprika, Garlic Powder, Parsley
3 tbsp – Avocado Oil
2 – Eggs, beaten

For the Sauce:
1 cup – Chicken Broth
1 cup – Heavy Cream
3 tbsp – Lemon Juice
1 tsp – Cornstarch, dissolved in hot water
1 tsp each: Salt, Garlic Powder, Onion Power

1:
Prepare all of the ingredients. Start water boiling for pasta.
2:
Place a pork loin filet between two pieces of plastic wrap and pound out until ½ in thick. Make a dredging station: On first plate, combine eggs, salt & pepper. On second plate, mix the flour and remaining pork seasonings. Then dredge the pork in the egg, then the flour. Repeat with all pieces.
3:
In a large sauté pan over medium-high heat, add the oil. Cook each breaded pork fillet for 5 minutes on each side.
4:
Add the pasta to the boiling water and cook as directed on the package.
5:
In a medium saucepan over medium heat, add the chicken broth and lemon juice and cook for 4 minutes. Then add the sauce seasoning and cornstarch, whisking until sauce starts to thicken. Keep whisking while adding the heavy cream. Reduce heat and allow to simmer for 5 minutes.

Plating Notes: In a shallow bowl, place a portion of pasta in center. Ladle cream sauce over pasta. Cut each piece of pork into strips and lay across the top of the pasta and drizzle additional sauce over top of pork. Garnish with parsley, if desired.

Variations: Use Chicken Breast instead of pork, increase cook time by 3 minutes on each side.

ZUPPA TOSCANA

Serves: 4-6   Prep Time: 15 min   Cook Time: 40
                              min

2 lb – Ground Italian Sausage
2 lb – Baby Red Potatoes, quartered
1 – White Onion, diced
5 – Garlic Cloves, minced
2 qt – Chicken Broth
4 cups – Kale, chopped
1 cup – Heavy Cream
1 cup – Parmesan Cheese, shredded
1 lb - Bacon, cut into ½-inch pieces
2 tsp each: Salt, Pepper, Basil, Red Pepper Flakes

1:
Prepare all of the ingredients.
2:
In a frying pan over medium-high heat, add bacon and cook until
crispy. Drain on paper towel and let cool.
3:
In a large pot over medium-high heat, add onion, garlic,
seasonings, and sausage. Cook for 5 minutes. Spoon out excess
grease. Then add broth, and potatoes. Reduce heat to medium,
cover and cook for 20 minutes.
4:
Add cream and parmesan cheese. Let cook another 5 minutes
then add kale and bacon.

Best served with a piece of Italian Bread smeared with
softened butter.

PORK CHOPS IN DIJON SAUCE

Serves: 6   Prep Time: 10 min   Cook Time: 30 min

For Pork Chops:
6 – Pork Chops
1 tsp each: Salt, ,Pepper, Rosemary 2 tbsp – Avocado
Oil

For Dijon Sauce:
3 tbsp – Butter
1 – Garlic Clove, minced
1 cup – Chicken or Vegetable Broth
1 cup – Heavy Cream
1/3 cup – Dijon Mustard
1 tsp each: Rosemary, Thyme

1:
Prepare all of the ingredients.
2:
In a large sauté pan over medium-high heat, add oil. Sprinkle pork
seasoning on pork and place them in pan. Cook on each side for 6
minutes. Remove from pan and keep warm.
3:
In the same pan, add butter and garlic, let melt. Whisk in
seasoning and broth. Cook for 2 minutes then whisk in heavy
cream. Let cook for 2 minutes then whisk in Dijon. Let cook
another 2 minutes then reduce heat to medium. Return pork
chops to pan, cover and let simmer for 5 additional minutes.

Side Dish Suggestion: Baked Cauliflower (recipe pg. 122) or Garlic
Parmesan Rice (recipe pg. 113)

TURKEY MEATBALLS WITH SUNDRIED TOMATO SAUCE

Serves: 4-6   Prep Time: 15 min   Cook Time: 25 min

2 lb – Egg Noodles

For the Meatballs:
1 lb - Ground Turkey
½ - White Onion, finely chopped
¼ cup – Flour (whole wheat or AP)
¼ cup - Fresh Sage, finely chopped
3 – Garlic Cloves, minced
1 tbsp each: Fresh Rosemary, Fresh Thyme, chopped
1 tsp each: Salt, Pepper, Red Pepper Flakes
2 tbsp – Avocado Oil

For the Sauce:
2 tbsp – Avocado Oil
2 15oz Cans – Coconut Milk, full-fat
1 cup – Chicken Broth
½ - White Onion, diced
1 tbsp each: Fresh Rosemary, Fresh Thyme, Fresh Sage, finely chopped
2 – Garlic Cloves, minced
2 tbsp: Sun-Dried Tomatoes (from a jar), chopped
1 tsp each: Salt, Pepper, Red Pepper Flakes

1:
Prepare all of the ingredients. Start water boiling for pasta. Preheat oven to 375deg.
2:
Drizzle large baking sheet with oil. In a mixing bowl, combine remaining meatball ingredients. Roll meatball mixture into 1-inch balls and space evenly on a baking sheet. Place in oven for 20 minutes.
3:
In a large sauté pan over medium-high heat, add oil, onions, and garlic, and cook for 4 minutes. Then add the chicken broth, fresh herbs and seasonings and cook for 4 minutes.
4:
Put the pasta into the boiling water and cook as directed on the package.
5:
Add the coconut milk and sun-dried tomatoes to the sauté pan, mixing thoroughly. When meatballs are done, remove from oven and add to the sauce.

Plating Notes: In a shallow bowl, place a portion of the pasta in the center of the bowl. Ladle the meatballs and sauce over the top of the pasta and garnish with red pepper flakes.

Variations: Use any kind of ground meat in place of turkey.

WHITE LASAGNA

Serves: 4-6   Prep Time: 15 min   Cook Time: 40 min

1 ½ lb – Chicken Breast
4 – Garlic Cloves, minced
1 lb – Lasagna Noodles
2 cup – Mozzarella Cheese, shredded
2 cups – Fresh Spinach
1 tbsp – Parsley, divided
2 cups – Ricotta Cheese
1 – Egg, beaten
1 cup – Parmesan Cheese, Shredded
1 tsp each: Garlic Powder, Basil, Oregano, Salt, Pepper

For the Alfredo Sauce:
¼ cup – Butter
¼ cup – Flour (AP, or Whole Wheat)
2 – Garlic Cloves, Minced
1 tsp – Salt
2 cup – Chicken Broth
1 cup – Heavy Cream
1 cup – Parmesan Cheese, shredded

1:
Prepare all of the ingredients. Preheat oven to 375 deg.
2:
In a saucepan over medium-high heat, add chicken breast, fresh garlic and just enough water to cover. Allow to boil for 15 minutes. Remove from water and shred chicken.
3:
In a medium saucepan over medium heat, melt butter and add garlic and salt. Let cook 3 minutes then add flour and whisk together. Allow to cook another 3 minutes, whisking occasionally. Slowly pour in the chicken broth while whisking. Allow to thicken slightly and then whisk in the heavy cream. Allow to cook for 3 minutes then whisk in the parmesan cheese, mixing until melted. Remove from heat.
4:
In a mixing bowl, combine Ricotta Cheese, Parmesan Cheese, egg, half of parsley and remaining seasonings.
5:
In a 13x9 baking dish begin to layer the lasagna as follows: alfredo sauce, lasagna noodles, ricotta mixture, chicken, spinach, mozzarella, alfredo sauce, lasagna noodles, ricotta mixture, chicken spinach, mozzarella, alfredo sauce, lasagna noodles, alfredo sauce, mozzarella, and remaining parsley. cover with foil and bake for 30 minutes. Remove foil and bake 10 more minutes. Let cool for 5 minutes before serving.

SPINACH ARTICHOKE STUFFED PORK CHOPS

Serves: 6   Prep Time: 10 min   Cook Time: 30 min

6 – Pork Chops, thick-cut, boneless
1 cup – Marinated Artichoke Hearts, chopped
1 cup – Frozen Spinach, thawed
1 cup – Cream Cheese
1 cup – Parmesan Cheese, shredded
2 – Garlic Cloves, minced
1 tsp each: Salt, Onion Powder, Parsley, Oregano
1 tbsp – Avocado Oil

1:
Prepare all of the ingredients. Preheat oven to 400deg.
2:
In a mixing bowl combine artichokes, spinach, cheeses, and garlic.
Sprinkle each side of pork chop with seasonings, then brush with
avocado oil. Make slit in the side of pork chop to make pocket.
Repeat with each pork chop. Evenly divide cheese mixture into
each pork chop.
3:
Place pork chops on cooking rack on baking sheet and place in
oven for 30 minutes.

Side Dish Suggestions: Garlic Parmesan Rice (recipe pg. 113) or
Roasted Potatoes & Cauliflower (recipe pg. 120)

STEAK & PROVOLONE PINWHEELS

Serves: 4-6   Prep Time: 15 min   Cook Time: 35 min

2lb — Steak Filets
1 cup - Fresh Spinach
8 slices — Provolone Cheese
1 tsp each: Salt, Pepper, Smoked Paprika, and Rosemary
1 tbsp — Avocado Oil

1:
Prepare all of the ingredients. Preheat oven to 425deg.
2:
Place one steak filet between two pieces of clear plastic wrap and flatten to ¼-in thickness. Sprinkle with seasonings, layer with provolone cheese slices and spinach. Tightly roll the filet, using a toothpick to hold in place. Brush with oil and place on cooking rack on a baking sheet. Repeat with remaining filets. Place in oven for 20 min.

Side Dish Suggestion: Potato Stacks (recipe pg. 114) or Honey Roasted Carrots (recipe pg. 127)

Plating Notes: Let the pinwheels rest for 5 minutes before cutting. Remove the toothpick and slice into 1-inch sections. On a flat plate, arrange 2-3 potato stacks on one side of the plate and 4-5 pinwheels on the other side of the plate. Garnish with favorite steak or BBQ sauce if desired.

You can find a recipe for Homemade Bourbon BBQ sauce on the website (homemadeonaweeknight.com).

CHICKEN CORDON BLEU CASSEROLE

Serves: 4-6   Prep Time: 10 min   Cook Time: 40 min

2 lb – Chicken Breast, cut into 1-inch chunks
8 oz - Ham Steak, cut into 1-inch chunks
¼ cup – Butter, melted
½ cup - Cream Cheese, softened
2 tbsp - Dijon Mustard
1 tbsp - White Wine
1 tbsp - Lemon Juice
1 tsp – Salt
8 slices - Swiss Cheese
1 tbsp - Parsley

1:
Prepare all of the ingredient. Preheat the oven to 350deg.
2:
In a 13x9 baking dish, put layer of chicken covering bottom.
Top with ham chunks.
3:
In a large bowl, mix melted butter, softened cream cheese,
white wine, mustard, lemon juice, and salt. Evenly spread over
the chicken & ham mixture, then top with swiss cheese slices.
4:
Cover baking pan with foil and bake for 35 minutes. Remove from
oven and increase oven temperature to broil. Remove foil,
sprinkle with parsley. Put back in oven for 2-3 minutes to crisp
top.

ROSEMARY & PAPRIKA PORK TENDERLOIN

Serves: 4-6   Prep Time: 15 min   Cook Time: 30 min

2lb – Pork Tenderloin
1 tbsp – Avocado Oil
1 tsp each: Rosemary, Salt, Pepper, Smoked Paprika, Parsley

1:
Prepare all of the ingredients. Preheat oven to 425deg.
2:
Place tenderloin on center of baking sheet. Brush oil over top then sprinkle seasoning mixture. Place in oven for 30 minutes. Let rest for 10 minutes before slicing to serve.

Side Dish Suggestion: Potatoes Au Gratin (recipe pg. 115) or Buttered Rice (recipe pg. 124)

CHICKEN & BROCCOLI ALFREDO

Serves: 4-6   Prep Time: 10 min   Cook Time: 30 min

1lb – Short Pasta (penne, rotini, cellentani)

For the Chicken:
1lb – Chicken Breast, cut into 1-inch chunks
2 cups – Broccoli Flowerets
2 tbsp – Avocado Oil
1 tsp each: Salt, Pepper, Oregano, Basil, Garlic Powder

For the Alfredo Sauce:
¼ cup – Butter
¼ cup – Flour (AP, Whole Wheat, Almond)
2 – Garlic Cloves, Minced
1 tsp – Salt
2 cup – Chicken Broth 1
cup – Heavy Cream
1 cup – Parmesan Cheese, shredded

1:
Prepare all of the ingredients. Start water boiling for pasta.
2:
In a medium saucepan over medium heat, melt butter and add garlic and salt. Let cook 3 minutes then add flour and whisk together. Allow to cook another 3 minutes, whisking occasionally. Slowly pour in the chicken broth while whisking. Allow to thicken slightly and then whisk in the heavy cream. Allow to cook for 3 minutes then whisk in the parmesan cheese, mixing until melted. Reduce heat to low, stirring occasionally.
3:
In a large saute pan over medium high heat, add oil. Sprinkle seasonings evenly over chicken. Add chicken to the sauté pan and cook for 8 min, stirring often.
4:
Add Pasta to boiling water and cook as directed on the package. When pasta is done, drain in colander and rinse with cool water to arrest cooking.
5:
Once there is no pink on the chicken, add the broccoli and mix together. Cook for 8 minutes more then stir in alfredo sauce.

Plating notes: There are two options – in a shallow pasta bowl, put a portion of pasta in the center of bowl and ladle sauce over top or return pasta to pot and pour sauce over, mixing together thoroughly before plating. Either method can be garnished with parmesan cheese and parsley, if desired.

ITALIAN CHICKEN & PASTA WITH RED PEPPER SAUCE

Serves: 6   Prep Time: 10 min   Cook Time: 45 min

1 ½ lb – Short Pasta (penne, farfalle, medium shells)

For Chicken:
6 - Chicken Breasts
1 tbsp – Avocado Oil
1 tsp each: Salt, Garlic Powder, Italian Seasoning

For Sauce:
1 tbsp – Avocado Oil
½ - Red Onion, diced
3 – Garlic Cloves, minced
1 tsp each: Salt, Italian Seasoning, Pepper
3 – Red Bell Peppers, chopped
2 cups – Chicken Broth
2 cups – Heavy Cream
1 cup – Parmesan Cheese, shredded

1:
Prepare all of the ingredients. Preheat oven to 400deg. Start water boiling for pasta.
2:
In a large sauté pan over medium-high heat, add oil, onions, garlic, and sauce seasonings. Let cook 5 minutes.
3:
Brush chicken with oil then sprinkle with chicken seasonings. Place on rack on cooking sheet and put into oven. Bake for 35 minutes. When done let rest 5 minutes before slicing into ½-inch pieces.
4:
Add red peppers to sauté pan and let cook for 10 minutes, stirring occasionally. Then add chicken broth, reduce heat to medium and cover pan. Let cook for 20 minutes.
5:
Add pasta to boiling water and cook as directed. When pasta is done, drain in colander and rinse with cool water to arrest cooking.
6:
Pour red peppers into a bowl and blend with an immersion blender until smooth. Return to pan and stir in heavy cream. Let cook 3 minutes then add in parmesan cheese.

Plating Notes: In a shallow bowl or flat plate, place portion of pasta in center. Ladle red pepper sauce over top, lay chicken slices across center and drizzle small amount of sauce over chicken. Garnish with parmesan cheese and parsley, if desired

SMOTHERED PORK CHOPS

Serves: 6   Prep Time: 10 min   Cook Time: 30 min

For Pork Chops:
6 – Pork Chops, boneless
1 tbsp – Avocado Oil
1 tsp each: Salt, Pepper, Garlic Powder, Thyme, Onion Powder

For Gravy:
1 tbsp – Avocado Oil
2 tbsp – Butter
2 tbsp – Flour (AP or Whole Wheat)
1 cup – Mushrooms. sliced
1 – Garlic Clove, minced
½ - White Onion, sliced rounds
½ cup – Dry White Wine
1 ½ cup – Chicken Broth
½ cup – Heavy Cream
1 tsp each: Salt, Pepper, Rosemary, Thyme

1:
Prepare all of the ingredients. Preheat oven to 400deg.
2:
In a large sauté pan over medium-high heat, add 1 tbsp of
avocado oil. Sprinkle both side of pork chops with seasonings
and add to pan. Cook 2 minutes on each side then transfer to
cooking sheet and put in oven for 20 minutes.
3:
In same sauté pan, reduce heat to medium and add 1 tablespoon
of avocado oil, butter, and garlic. Cook 2 minutes then add onions
and mushrooms, let cook another 2 minutes. Add flour to pan and
thoroughly combine. Add white wine and cook for 2 minutes. Stir
in chicken broth and let cook, stirring frequently, for 5 minutes.
Stir in seasonings and heavy cream. Reduce heat to medium-low
and simmer until pork chops are ready to serve.

Side Dish Suggestions: Whipped Garlic Cauliflower (recipe pg. 112)

Plating Notes: On a plate, place a portion of whipped cauliflower
just off center. Lay Pork Chop half on cauliflower half off. Ladle
gravy over entire plate.

STEAK BUNDLES

Serves: 4-6   Prep Time: 15 min   Cook Time: 20 min

2 Lb – Flank Steak, cut in 6-inch pieces
1 – Green Bell Peppers, cut in ¼-in strips
1 – Red Bell Peppers, cut in ¼-in strips
1 – Yellow Bell Peppers, cut in ¼-in strips
18 – Asparagus Spears, ends cut
2 tsp each: Salt, Pepper, Garlic Powder, Onion Powder,
Paprika, Parsley
2 tbsp – Avocado Oil
4 tbsp - Butter

1:
Prepare all of the ingredients.
2:
Lay a piece of steak flat and sprinkle with seasoning mixture on
both sides. In the center pile up two pieces of each vegetable. Pull
up the sides of the steak and secure with a toothpick. Brush
outside of steak and vegetables with avocado oil. Repeat with
remaining steak pieces.
3:
In a large sauté pan over medium-high heat, add butter. Once
melted add the steak bundles, toothpick side down and sear for 3
minutes. Turn bundles over and cook for 3 more minutes while
spooning butter over top of bundles frequently.

Side Dish Suggestions: Potato Stacks (recipe pg. 114) or Corn
Salad (recipe pg. 117)

Variations: Use thin-sliced Chicken Breast instead of Steak.
Prepare the same way but cook for 8 minutes longer on each side.

MUSHROOM CHICKEN

Serves: 6   Prep Time: 10 min   Cook Time: 30 min

6 – Chicken Breast, thin sliced
2 cups – Baby Bella Mushrooms, sliced
3 – Garlic Cloves, minced
2 tbsp – Avocado Oil
4 tbsp – Butter
2 tbsp – Corn Starch
2 cups – Chicken Broth
½ cup – Red Cooking Wine
1 tsp each: Salt, Pepper
½ cup – Flour (AP or Whole Wheat)
1 cup – Mozzarella Cheese, shredded
1 cup – Parmesan Cheese, shredded
3 – Scallions, sliced
1 tbsp – Parsley

1:
Prepare all of the ingredients. Preheat oven to 400deg.
2:
On a flat plate, combine flour, salt, and pepper. Dredge chicken in flour mixture evenly on both sides.
3: In a large sauté pan over medium-high heat, add avocado oil, garlic, and mushrooms. Cook, stirring frequently, for 5 minutes. Remove mushrooms from pan. Add 2 tablespoons butter to pan and let melt. Cook each piece of chicken for 3 minutes on each side and remove from pan.
4:
In the same pan, melt remaining butter. Add chicken broth and wine, let cook for 3 minutes. Then stir in cornstarch (mixed with 2 tbsp warm water). Once thickened remove from heat.
5:
Place chicken in a 13x9 baking dish and pour pan sauce over top. Next put mushroom mixture over the chicken. Combine the cheeses and sprinkle over top of chicken and mushrooms. Then sprinkle with scallions and parsley. Put in oven and bake for 15 minutes.

Side Dish Suggestion: Garlic Parmesan Rice (recipe pg. 113) or Baked Cauliflower (recipe pg. 122)

CREAMY ASPARAGUS CHICKEN

Serves: 6   Prep Time: 10 min   Cook Time: 35 min

For the Chicken:
6 – Chicken Thighs, bone-in
1 lb – Asparagus, cut in 3-inch pieces
1 tsp each: Salt, Pepper, Garlic Powder, Rosemary,
Thyme
2 tbsp -Avocado Oil

For Pan Sauce:
¼ cup – Butter
3 tbsp – Flour (AP or Whole Wheat)
1 cup – Chicken Broth
2 cups – Heavy Cream
3 – Garlic Cloves, minced
1 tsp each: Salt, Pepper, Rosemary, Thyme, Onion Powder
1 cup – Parmesan Cheese, shredded

1:
Prepare all of the ingredients.
2:
Season chicken thighs with chicken seasonings. In a large sauté
pan over medium-high heat, add oil. Add chicken to pan and cook
for 8 minutes on each side. Remove chicken from pan and keep
warm.
3:
In same pan add butter and garlic, cook for 2 minutes. Add flour
and sauce seasonings and cook for 2 minutes. Whisk in chicken
broth and cook for 3 minutes. Whisk in heavy cream and cook for
3 minutes. Stir in parmesan cheese and cook for 3 minutes. Add in
asparagus pieces and return chicken to pan. Cover and cook for
10 more minutes.

Side Dish Suggestions: Baked Cauliflower (recipe pg. 122) or
Buttered Rice (recipe pg. 124)

PARMESAN CRUSTED PORK CHOPS

Serves: 6   Prep Time: 15 min   Cook Time: 20 min

6 – Pork Chops, boneless
2 – Eggs, beaten
2 cups – Parmesan Cheese, shredded
¾ cup – Butter
1 tsp each: Salt, Garlic Powder, Parsley, Basil

1:
Prepare all of the ingredients.
2:
Make a dredging station: On first plate, combine eggs and seasoning. On second plate, put cheese. First dredge pork chop in egg then cheese. Repeat with remaining pork chops
3:
In a large sauté pan over medium-high heat, melt butter. Put pork chop in pan and cook on each side for 8 minutes.

Side Dish Suggestions: Pasta in Red Sauce (recipe pg. 128)

Variations: Make with thin-sliced Chicken Breast instead of Pork Chops.

ETHNIC ADVENTURES

LEMON COCONUT CHICKEN

Serves: 4-6   Prep Time: 10 min   Cook Time: 25 min

2 lb - Chicken Breasts, thin sliced
2 cups - Basmati Rice
2 qts - Chicken Broth
1 15oz can - Coconut Milk, full-fat
1 cup - Summer Squash, cubed
1 cup - Cilantro, chopped
1 - White Onion, diced
2 - Garlic Cloves, minced
1 tbsp - Fresh Ginger, grated
4 - Lemons - 3 for juice & 1 for sliced garnish
2 tbsp – Avocado Oil
1 tsp each: Seal Salt, Pepper

1:
Prepare all of the ingredients.
2:
In a pan over medium-high heat, add rice and 1 quart of chicken broth. Cover and let cook for 15 minutes. Remove pan from heat and leave lid on until ready to serve.
3:
In a large sauté pan over medium-high heat, add 1 tbsp oil. Season the chicken breasts with salt and pepper then pan fry each piece for 7 minutes per side. Set chicken aside.
4:
Add the remaining oil to the pan and add onion, garlic, ginger, and summer squash. Cook, stirring frequently, for 5 minutes. Add chicken broth to the veggies and let simmer for 5 minutes. Then add coconut milk, lemon juice and 1/2 of the cilantro. Let cook for another 5 minutes. Slice the chicken into strips.

Plating Notes: Put a portion of rice in the bottom of a shallow bowl. Lay the sliced chicken over the top of the rice. Then ladle the Lemon Coconut sauce with veggies over the top of all of it. Sprinkle chopped cilantro over the top and then lay 2 lemon slices atop the chicken slices.

KOREAN BEEF RICE BOWL

Serves: 4-6   Prep time: 15 min   Cook Time: 25 min

2 lb – Ground Beef
½ - Yellow Onion, diced
2 – Garlic Cloves, minced
2 tbsp – Fresh Ginger, grated
2 tbsp – Avocado Oil
4 tbsp – Coco Aminos or Soy Sauce
2 tbsp – Fish Sauce
2 tbsp – Sriracha
1 tsp each: Salt, Black Ground Pepper, Red Pepper Flakes,
Parsley, Sesame Seeds
4 – Scallions, diced
1 – Buttered Rice (recipe pg. 124)
1 – Asian Sweet & Spicy Cucumber Salad (recipe pg. 118)

1:
Prepare all of the ingredients.
2:
In a small bowl combine coco aminos, Sriracha, fish sauce and
seasonings. In a large sauté pan over medium-high heat, add oil,
onions, and garlic. Cook for 2 minutes and add ground beef,
ginger, and sauce mixture. Cook for 10 minutes.

Plating Notes: In a shallow bowl, place a portion of rice in center.
Spoon a portion of beef over top of rice, Place a portion of the
cucumber salad to one side of the bowl and sprinkle dish with
scallions. Garnish with sesame seeds, if desired.

CREAMY RED ENCHILADAS

Serves: 6   Prep Time: 15 min   Cook Time: 30 min

1 15oz can - Tomato Sauce
1 qt - Chicken Broth 3
tbsp - Avocado Oil
1 cup - Sour Cream
1/2 - White Onion, minced
3 – Garlic Cloves, minced
2 tsp each: Smoked Paprika, Ground Cumin
1 tsp each: Salt, Black Pepper
15 – Tortillas, Fajita-sized (flour or corn)
1lb – Cooked Filling meat of choice (chicken, beef, pork), optional
2 cups – Sharp Cheddar, shredded

1:
Prepare all of the ingredients. Preheat Oven to 375deg.
2:
In a saucepan over medium-high heat, add oil, onion, and garlic, and cook for 3 minutes. Add the broth, and all the seasonings. Whisk together until all the oil is incorporated and let it cook for 3 minutes. Reduce the heat to medium and slowly whisk in the Tomato Sauce. Once a smooth sauce, let it come just to a bubble. Using a slotted spoon, remove any larger pieces of onion and garlic that did not break down. Then reduce heat to low and simmer while you prepare your enchiladas.
4:
Fill each tortilla with desired meat and small amount of cheese and line them up in a 13x9 baking dish.
5:
Whisk in the sour cream into the red sauce. Let simmer for 2-3 minutes then pour over your pan of enchiladas. Sprinkle remaining cheese on top of the sauce. Bake for 30 minutes. Allow to cook about 5 minutes before serving.

Side Dish Suggestions: for Rice & Beans (recipe pg. 129)

Variation: Make cheese enchiladas by omitting filling meat and adding another two cups of cheese.

RAVIOLI BAKE

Serves: 4-6   Prep Time: 10 min   Cook Time: 45 min

2 lb – Ravioli, pre-made (fresh or frozen)
2 cup – Mozzarella Cheese, shredded
2 cup – Fresh Spinach
1 cup – Parmesan Cheese, shredded
1 cup – Ricotta Cheese
1 tsp each: Garlic Powder, Onion Powder, Oregano, Basil
1 – Egg

For the Alfredo Sauce:
¼ cup – Butter
¼ cup – Flour (AP, Whole Wheat, Almond)
2 – Garlic Cloves, minced
1 tsp – Salt
2 cup – Chicken Broth
1 cup – Heavy Cream
1 cup – Parmesan Cheese, shredded

1:
Prepare all of the ingredients. Preheat oven to 400deg
2:
In a medium saucepan over medium heat, melt butter and add garlic and salt. Let cook 3 minutes then add flour and whisk together. Allow to cook another 3 minutes, whisking occasionally. Slowly pour in the chicken broth while whisking. Allow to thicken slightly and then whisk in the heavy cream. Allow to cook for 3 minutes then whisk in the parmesan cheese, mixing until melted. Remove from heat.
3:
In a bowl, mix Ricotta Cheese, seasonings, egg, and parmesan cheese.
4:
In a 13x9 pan, coat the bottom with a thin layer of Alfredo sauce. Make a layer of ravioli topped with a layer of Ricotta mix, followed by a layer of Spinach, a layer of Mozzarella Cheese. Then start over with Alfredo sauce and make all the layers again for 3 full layers. Cover with foil and bake for 25 min. Remove foil and let bake 5 more minutes. Let cool for 5 minutes before serving.

LAMB PITAS

Serves: 6   Prep Time: 15 min   Cook Time: 40 min

1 ½ lb – Lamb Roast
1 tsp each: Salt, Pepper, Dill, Smoked Paprika, Garlic Powder
6 – Pitas
1 cup – Arugula or Micro Greens
1 cup – Cherry Tomatoes, halved
1 – Tzatziki Sauce (recipe pg. 116)
1 cup – Feta Cheese, crumbled

1:
Prepare all ingredients. Preheat Grill or Smoker to 400deg
2:
Season Lamb roast and wrap in foil. Place on grill, turning every 10 minutes for 40 minutes. When done, remove from foil. Let rest 5 minutes then cut into bite sized pieces.
3:
In last ten minutes of grilling, take the pitas out to the grill and lightly grill on each side.

Side Dish Suggestion: Greek Cucumber Salad (recipe pg. 118)

Plating Notes: On a plate, start with a grilled pita, place a serving of lamb, a spoonful of tzatziki sauce, some greens, tomatoes, and feta cheese. Serve cucumber salad on the side.

HONEY GARLIC CHICKEN

Serves: 4-6   Prep Time: 10 min   Cook time: 25 min

1 tbsp - Avocado Oil
3 – Scallions, sliced
1 tsp – Sesame Seeds, for garnish
For the Chicken:
1½ lb – Chicken Thigh, boneless, skinless, cut into 1-inch chunks
¼ cup – Honey
¼ cup – Coco Aminos
1 – Garlic Cloves, minced
1 tsp – Fish Sauce
1 tsp – Ginger Powder

1:
Prepare all of the ingredients.
2:
In a mixing bowl, combine all ingredients for the chicken until
well coated. In a large sauté pan over medium-high heat, add the
oil. Add marinated chicken (with marinating liquids) and cook for
5 minutes, stirring frequently. Reduce heat to medium- low and
cook another 10 minutes.

Side Dish Suggestion: Garlic Noodles (recipe pg. 119) or Buttered
Rice (recipe pg. 124)

Plating Notes: In a shallow bowl or on a flat plate, place a portion
of the garlic noodles or rice. Then place a portion of Honey Garlic
Chicken on top. Garnish with sesame seeds and scallions.

To increase the flavor, let chicken marinate for 30 minutes (up
to 24 hours, in the refrigerator, before cooking).

STEAK TACOS

Serves: 6   Prep Time: 15 min   Cook Time: 30 min

1 ½ lb – Top Round Steak Filets, flattened to ¾ inch

1 tsp each: Cumin, Garlic Powder, Chili Powder, Salt

2 tbsp – Avocado Oil

12 – Tortillas, fajita size (flour or corn)

1 cup – Romaine Lettuce, shredded

1 cup – Sharp Cheddar Cheese, shredded

8 oz – Sour Cream

1 – Restaurant Style Salsa (recipe pg. 123)

1:

Prepare all of the ingredients. Preheat oven to 450deg. Preheat Griddle to high heat.

2:

On a baking sheet with a cooking rack, half of sprinkle steak seasoning on steak, then brush half of oil over seasoning. Flip steaks over and repeat. Place on top rack of oven and cook for 15 minutes. Remove to cutting board and let rest at least 5 minutes before cutting into bite-size pieces.

3:

Cook the tortillas on the griddle on each side for 1-2 minutes. As soon as they are cooked, fold in half, and put cheese in fold. Then layer in steak, lettuce, salsa, and sour cream.

Variations: Use chicken (cook same way, adding 15 minutes cook time). Use Shrimp (cook same way but decrease cooking by 5 minutes).

CHICKEN COCONUT CURRY

Serves: 4-6   Prep Time: 15 min   Cook Time: 40 min

For Rice:
2 cups – Basmati Rice
1 qt – Chicken Broth
¼ cup – Cilantro, chopped

For Curry:
2 lbs – Baby Potatoes, quartered
¼ - Red Onion, diced
1 tbsp – Avocado Oil
3 – Garlic Cloves, minced
2 tsp – Fresh Ginger, grated
2 lbs – Chicken Tenderloins, cut into in 1-inch chunks
2 qts – Chicken Broth
1 15oz can – Coconut Milk, full fat
3 tbsp – Curry Powder (equal parts coriander, turmeric, cumin, mustard seed, ginger, cayenne, and fenugreek)

1:
Prepare all of the ingredients.
2:
In a large pot over medium-high heat, add oil, onion, ginger, and garlic. Let cook for 3 minutes. Then add chicken chunks and cook until no longer pink on outside. Add chicken broth, curry powder, and potatoes. Bring to a boil, reduce heat to medium and cover pot. Cook for 15 minutes then stir in coconut milk. Cook, uncovered, for 10 minutes more.
3:
In a separate pot over medium-high heat, add rice, cilantro, and chicken broth. Cover and let cook for 15-20 minutes. Remove from heat and leave lid on until ready to serve.

Plating Notes: In a shallow bowl, put a serving of rice to one side. Ladle Curry into bowl, leaving most of rice visible. Garnish with cilantro.

TACO PASTA

Serves: 4-6   Prep Time: 5 min   Cook Time: 25 min

1 ½ lb – Short Pasta (shells, penne, rotini)
2 lb – Ground Turkey
1 tsp each: Chili Powder, Garlic Powder, Salt, Cumin
1 tbsp – Avocado Oil

For Cheese Sauce:
3 tbsp – Butter
3 tbsp – Flour (AP or Almond)
2 cups – Chicken Broth
1 cup – Heavy Cream
1 9oz can – Tomato Paste
1 7oz can – Green Chilis, diced
2 cups – Cheddar Cheese, shredded
1 tsp each: Salt, Chili Powder, Garlic Powder, Cumin

1:
Prepare all of the ingredients. Start water boiling for pasta.
2:
In a large sauté pan over medium-high heat, add avocado oil, ground turkey and seasonings. Cook fully then remove from pan. Add pasta to boiling water and cook as directed on the package.
3:
In the same sauté pan, reduce heat to medium and add butter. Once melted add flour and whisk together. Let cook for 2 minutes then whisk in chicken broth. Let cook for 2 minutes then whisk in heavy cream. Let cook for 2 minutes then whisk in tomato paste, seasonings and green chilis. Let cook for 2 minutes then whisk in cheese. Let cook for 2 minutes then return turkey to sauce and reduce heat to low. Let simmer while draining pasta.

Variations: Use ground beef instead of ground turkey. Use pickled jalapenos instead of green chilis

Plating: Serve with sauce poured over pasta on plate or return pasta to pan and combine with sauce before serving.

SHRIMP FRIED RICE

Serves: 4-6   Prep Time: 10 min   Cook Time: 30 min

2 cups – Short Grain Rice
1 qt – Chicken Broth
1 ½ lb – Medium Shrimp, cooked, peeled, deveined, tall-off
1 cup – Pea & Carrot mix, frozen
3 – Scallions, sliced thin
2 tbsp – Avocado Oil
2 tbsp – Coco Aminos or Soy Sauce
4 – Eggs, beaten

1:
Prepare all of the ingredients
2:
It is best to prepare the rice the day before, or at least earlier in the day, so that it is completely cooled. In a saucepan over medium heat, add rice and chicken broth. Cover and cook for 15 minutes. Remove from heat and leave lid on until ready to serve.
3:
In a large sauté pan over medium-high heat, add avocado oil. Add cooled rice and stir frequently for 3 minutes. Stir in coco aminos and cook for 2 minutes. Stir in Pea & Carrot mix and half of the scallions. Cook for 3 minutes then stir in Shrimp.
4:
Make a well in the center of the rice and pour eggs into sauté pan. Stir frequently while scrambling eggs in center of pan before mixing In. Once eggs are mostly cooked combine entire contents of pan.

Plating: Place a portion of the Fried Rice on a plate and top with remaining scallions. Garnish with sesame seeds, if desired.

Variations: Use chicken cut into 1-inch chunks, however, add to pan at the same time as coco aminos.

ONE POT SPANISH CHICKEN & RICE

Serves: 6   Prep Time: 10 min   Cook Time: 35 min

6 - Chicken Thighs, bone-in
1 tsp each: Salt, Smoked Paprika, Oregano
2 cups – Long Grain Rice
4 tbsp – Avocado Oil
½ - Yellow Onion, diced
2 – Garlic cloves, minced
1 15oz can – Diced Tomatoes
1 7oz can – Green Chilies
1 qt – Chicken Broth
½ cup – Fresh Parsley, chopped
1 tbsp – Lemon Juice

1:
Prepare all of the ingredients
2:
In a large sauté pan over medium-high heat, add half of oil.
Sprinkle chicken with seasonings and cook on each side for 5
minutes then remove from pan.
3:
Add remaining oil, onions, and garlic to pan and sauté for 2
minutes. Add rice to pan and sauté for 3 minutes. Stir in broth,
parsley, tomatoes, green chilies, and lemon juice. Bring just to a
boil.
4:
Return chicken to pan, reduce heat to medium and cover pan.
Cook for 15 minutes.

HOMEMADE ENCHILADAS

Serves: 6   Prep Time: 5 min   Cook Time: 35 min

For the Sauce:
2 6oz cans - Tomato Paste
1 qt - Chicken or Vegetable Broth
3 tbsp - Avocado Oil
¼ cup - Flour (AP or Whole Wheat)
2 tsp each: Garlic Powder, Onion Powder, Chili Powder, Cumin
1tsp each: Salt, Black Pepper

For the Enchiladas:
16 – Flour Tortillas, fajita size
1 lb – Cooked Filling Meat (chicken, beef, pork), shredded
2 cup – Sharp Cheese, shredded

1:
Prepare all of the ingredients. Preheat oven to 375deg.
2:
In a saucepan over medium-high heat, add the oil, tomato paste, flour, and all seasonings. Whisk together until all the oil is incorporated to make a smooth paste. Allow to cook for 3 minutes.* Flavor Note: If more heat is desired, add a half teaspoon of Cayenne Pepper.
3:
Reduce heat to medium and slowly whisk in the broth until the sauce is smooth. Cook for 3 minutes then reduce heat to low and simmer until ready to use.
4:
Fill each tortilla with meat and a small amount of cheese, then roll up and placing in a 13x9 glass baking dish. Once all tortillas are filled, pour the enchilada sauce over the top. Sprinkle remaining cheese over the top. Put in oven for 20 minutes. Allow to cool at least 5 minutes before serving.

Side Dish Suggestion: Rice & Beans (recipe pg. 129)

SWEET & SPICY PORK CHOPS

Serves: 6   Prep Time: 10 min   Cook Time: 25 min

6 – Pork Chops, boneless
1 9oz – Tomato Paste
1 cup – Chicken Broth
2 tbsp – Avocado Oil
2 – Garlic Cloves, minced
½ cup – Sriracha
¼ cup – Honey
1 tsp each: Salt, Pepper, Onion Powder, Parsley

1:
Prepare all of the ingredients. Preheat oven to 400deg.
2:
In a small saucepan over medium heat, add 1 tbsp oil and garlic.
Sauté for 2 minutes then whisk in chicken broth and tomato paste
until smooth. Let cook 2 minutes then whisk Sriracha and honey
and cook another minute. Reduce heat to low and let simmer,
stirring occasionally.
3:
Sprinkle seasonings on both sides of pork chops and then brush
with remaining oil. Place on cooking rack on baking sheet and
place in oven for 15 minutes. Remove from oven and brush pork
chops with Sweet & Spicy Sauce, then return to oven for 5
minutes more.

Suggested Side Dish: Garlic Noodles (recipe pg. 119)

HUEVOS RANCHEROS

Serves: 6   Prep Time: 15 min   Cook Time: 25 min

12 – Eggs
4 tbsp - Butter
2 15oz can – Refried Beans
1 cup – Milk
2 tsp each: Salt, Pepper, Garlic Powder, Cumin
24 – Corn Tortillas, fajita size
3 cups – Cheddar Cheese, finely shredded
4 2 – Avocados, sliced

For the Sauce:
¼ cup – Avocado Oil
½ cup – Chicken Broth
2 – Roma Tomatoes, diced
2 – Garlic Cloves, minced
½ - White Onion, diced
½ cup – Cilantro, chopped
2 – Chipotle Peppers in Adobo Sauce, diced
3 tbsp – Lime Juice
1 tsp each: Salt, Pepper, Oregano, Chili Powder

1:
Prepare all of the ingredients. Preheat Griddle to high heat.
2:
In a saucepan over medium-high heat, add all ingredients for sauce and cook for 5 minutes, stirring often. Reduce heat to medium low and simmer for 10 more minutes. Then transfer to bowl and let cool.
3:
In another saucepan over medium heat, add beans, cumin, garlic powder and half of salt and pepper. Let cook 3 minutes then add milk and half of cheese. Stir thoroughly and reduce heat to medium low.
4:
In a large frying pan over medium-high heat, melt butter. Fry eggs (two per serving) to "over medium".
5:
Using an immersion blender, blitz the sauce mixture until well combined.
6:
Cook tortillas on griddle – 1 minute on each side.

Plating Notes: On a plate, place 2 tortillas. Spread two spoonfuls of beans on each, top with a spoonful of sauce, cheese and then a fried egg. Place 3 slices of avocado on the side. Garnish with chopped cilantro, if desired.

CHICKEN SOUVLAKI

Serves: 4-6   Prep Time: 45 min   Cook Time: 20
                                    min

2 lb – Chicken Tenderloins
4 tbsp – Avocado Oil
2 tbsp – White Vinegar
3 – Garlic Cloves, minced
3 tbsp – Lemon Juice
1 tbsp each: Oregano, Parsley
1 tsp each: Salt, Pepper, Cumin, Red Pepper Flakes
1 – Batch Tzatziki Sauce (recipe pg. 116), for dipping

20 Skewers

1:
Prepare all of the ingredients. Preheat grill or grill pan to
medium-high heat.
2:
In a large bowl, combine all ingredients except Tzatziki Sauce. Let
chicken marinate for at least 30 minutes in the refrigerator.
3:
Weave one tenderloin on to each skewer. Place skewers on grill
and cook for 20 minutes, turning 3 times.

Side Dish Suggestions: Greek Cucumber Salad (recipe pg. 118) or
Pasta Salad (recipe pg. 126)

Variations: Use Lamb Roast, cut into 1 ½ inch pieces, in place of
chicken. Put 4-6 pieces on each skewer.

SHEET PAN CHICKEN FAJITAS

Serves: 4-6   Prep Time: 15 min   Cook Time: 30 min

2 lb – Chicken Tenderloins
1 – White Onion, sliced
1 – Red Bell Pepper, sliced
1 – Green Bell Pepper, sliced
1 – Yellow Bell Pepper, sliced
3 – Garlic Cloves, minced
2 tbsp – Avocado Oil
2 tbsp – Lime Juice
2 tsp each: Salt, Chili Powder, Cumin, Parsley
1 – Salsa of Choice (recipe pg. 123)
12-18 – Tortillas, fajita size
1 cup – Sour Cream
1 cup – Cheddar Cheese, finely shredded
½ cup – Fresh Cilantro, chopped
2 – Limes, cut into wedges

1:
Prepare all of the ingredients. Preheat oven to 400deg.
2:
In a large bowl combine chicken, onion, garlic, peppers, oil, lime juice and seasonings. Spread evenly on large baking sheet and place in oven for 30 minutes.
3:
Wrap stack of tortillas in foil and place in oven for last 10 minutes of bake time.

Plating Notes: On a large plate, place a portion of fajita mix and tortillas. On a smaller plate, arrange assortment of sour cream, salsa, cheese, lime wedges and cilantro.

Variations: Use Medium Shrimp or Flank Steak cut into ½- in strips – reduce baking time by 10 minutes.

Side Dish Suggestion: Rice & Beans (recipe pg. 129)

IRISH BEEF STEW

Serves: 4-6   Prep Time: 15 min   Cook Time: 45 min

1 ½ lb - Beef Chuck Roast, cut into 1 ½-inch pieces
1 – White Onion, cut into in 1 ½-inch pieces
1 lb – Baby Carrots
2 lb – Baby Potatoes, halved
2 cups – Peas, fresh or frozen
2 tbsp – Avocado Oil
1 ½ qt – Beef Broth
1 tbsp – Thyme
1 tbsp – Tarragon
1 tsp each: Salt, Pepper

1:
Prepare all of the ingredients.
2:
In a large stock pot over medium-high heat, add oil. Sprinkle beef pieces with salt and pepper then add to pan. Cook until all sides are browned, about 5 minutes. Add onions and cook another 3 minutes. Then add broth, potatoes, carrots, and thyme. Bring just to a boil, cover, and reduce heat to medium heat. Cook for 20 minutes more.
3:
Remove lid and stir in peas and tarragon. Cook another 10 minutes.

Variations: Use Lamb roast instead of beef and extend the first cooking time by 10 minutes.

IBERIAN CHICKEN & POTATOES

Serves: 6   Prep Time: 15 min   Cook Time: 45 min

6 – Chicken Thighs, bone-in
1 lb – Baby Potatoes, halved
1 – White Onion, diced
2 tbsp – Lemon Juice
2 tbsp – Fresh Parsley, chopped
4 tbsp – Avocado Oil
3 – Garlic Cloves, minced
2 tbsp – Brown Sugar
2 tsp each: Salt, Pepper, Smoked Paprika

1:
Prepare all of the ingredients. Preheat Oven to 400deg.
2:
In a bowl, mix chicken, lemon juice, parsley and half of seasonings.
In a large sauté pan over medium-high heat, add 2 tablespoons of
oil. Cook chicken on each side for 5 minutes. Remove chicken from
heat and add remaining oil.
3:
Add garlic and onions to pan and cook for 3 minutes. Add
remaining seasonings, potatoes, and brown sugar. Stir thoroughly
and cook for 5 minutes.
4:
In a 13x9 baking dish, transfer potato mixture evenly across
bottom. Place chicken thighs evenly on top of potatoes. Place in
oven and cook for 30 minutes.

HAWAIIAN LOCO MOCO

Serves: 6   Prep Time: 15 min   Cook Time: 20 min

1 – Buttered Rice (recipe pg. 124)
6 – Eggs
2 tbsp – Butter
½ cup – Cilantro, chopped
½ cup - Sriracha

For Gravy:
2 tbsp – Butter
2 tbsp – Flour (AP or Whole Wheat)
1 qt – Beef Bone Broth

For Patties:
1 lb – Ground Beef
1 lb – Ground Pork
1 – Egg, beaten
½ - yellow onion, minced
4 tbsp - Butter
2 tsp each: Salt, Pepper, Garlic Powder, Smoked Paprika, Parsley

1:
Prepare all of the ingredients.
2:
In a mixing bowl, combine ingredients for patties and form
into six 4-inch patties. In a large sauté pan over medium-high
heat, melt butter for patties. Cook patties for 5 minutes on
each side. Remove from pan and keep warm.
3:
In a separate frying pan over medium-high heat, melt butter
for eggs. Fry each egg over medium.
4:
In the pan the patties were cooked in, melt butter for gravy.
Whisk in flour, scrapping up bits on bottom of pan. Let cook for 2
minutes then whisk in broth. Cook for 3 minutes then reduce heat
to medium low.

Plating Notes: On a plate, place a portion of rice. In the center
place one patty and ladle gravy over top. Place egg on top of
patty and garnish with cilantro and drizzle of Sriracha.

SPANISH CHICKEN STEW

Serves: 6   Prep Time: 15 min   Cook Time: 35 min

6 – Chicken Thigh, bone-in, skin removed
2 tbsp – Avocado Oil
1 – Red Bell Pepper, cut into ½-inch strips
1 – Yellow Bell Pepper, cut into ½-inch strips
3 – Garlic Cloves, minced
1 28oz can – Crushed Tomatoes
1 cup – Chicken Broth
1 tsp each: Salt, Pepper, Red Pepper Flakes
1 – Buttered Rice (recipe pg. 124)

1:
Prepare all of the ingredients.
2:
In a large sauté pan over medium-high heat, add oil and garlic.
Sprinkle chicken with salt and pepper then add to pan. Cook on
each side for 4 minutes.
3:
Mix in bell peppers and cook for 3 minutes. Then add tomatoes,
broth, and pepper flakes. Cover and cook for 15 minutes more.

Plating notes: In a shallow bowl, place a portion of rice. Spoon
stew over top and garnish with parsley, if desired.

SOUPS, SALADS & BOWLS

CHEESY CHICKEN CORN CHOWDER

Serves 6-8   Prep Time: 10 min   Cook Time: 35 min

1 ½ b – Chicken Breasts , cubed
1 – Red Onion, minced
2 – Garlic Cloves, minced
2 lb - Baby Potatoes, quartered
1 lb – Bacon, cut into ½-inch pieces
1 can - Sweet Corn, drained
1 qt - Chicken Broth
1 cup – Heavy Cream
2 cup - Sharp Cheddar, shredded
1 tsp each: Salt, Pepper, Thyme, Rosemary, Parsley
1 tbsp -Avocado Oil

1:
Prepare all of the ingredients.
2:
In a soup pot over medium heat, add oil, onion, and garlic and cook for 3 minutes. Add chicken, salt, and pepper. Cook for 5 minutes, while stirring frequently.
3:
Add chicken broth and remaining seasonings. Bring to a boil and then add potatoes. Cook at a boil for 5 minutes then reduce the heat to medium. Cook 10 minutes more.
4:
In a frying pan over medium-high heat, add bacon. Cook until crispy and remove to a paper towel covered plate.
5:
Add corn to soup pot. Then add heavy cream mixing continuously so that it does not curdle. Let cook 3 more minutes than start adding the cheese - 1/2 cup at a time - mixing continuously. Simmer on medium low for 5 minutes more.

Plating Notes: Keep the bacon crispy by placing a small amount in the bottom of a shallow bowl. Then ladle the soup over the top. Last, garnish with more bacon, cheese, and parsley.

THAI INSPIRED COCONUT SHRIMP SOUP

Serves: 4-6   Prep Time: 10 min   Cook Time: 25 min

1 lb - Medium Shrimp, raw, peeled, deveined
2 qt – Chicken Broth, divided
2 cup - Basmati Rice,
4 tbsp – Avocado Oil
1 - Red Bell Pepper, cut into 1-inch pieces
1 - Yellow Onion, diced
3 - Garlic Cloves, minced
1 tbsp – Fresh Ginger, grated
2 15oz cans - Coconut Milk, full fat
1 tbsp - Lime Juice
½ cup - Cilantro, chopped
1 tsp each: Salt, Pepper, and Red Pepper Flakes

1:
Prepare all of the ingredients.
2:
In a pan over medium-high heat, add rice and 1 quart of chicken
broth. Cover and let cook for 15 minutes. Remove pan from heat
and leave lid on until ready to serve.
3:
In a large sauté pan over medium-high heat, add 2 tbsp oil. Add
shrimp and seasoning. Cook until shrimp is just done, remove
from the pan and set aside.
4:
In a large pot over medium heat, add remaining oil and onion.
Cook 2 minutes then add garlic. Cook 2 minutes , then add ginger
and cook 2 minutes. Add the bell peppers and cook 4 minutes.
5:
Add remaining chicken broth. Then whisk in coconut milk.
Increase the heat to medium-high and bring to a rolling boil.
Allow to boil for 2 minutes then reduce heat to medium. Stir in
lime juice, cilantro and add back shrimp.

Plating Notes: In a shallow bowl, place a mound of the cooked rice
in the center. Ladle the soup over the top of the rice. Garnish with
a sprinkle of cilantro and red pepper flakes.

ASIAN SOUP & SALAD

Serves: 6   Prep Time: 15 min   Cook Time: 25 min

For the Soup:
2 qts – Chicken or Beef Broth
4 -Scallions, sliced
2 cups - Carrots, shredded
1 cup - Snap Peas, with ends chopped
1 lb - Thin Spaghetti Noodles
6 – Eggs
¼ cup each: Rice Vinegar, Fish Sauce, Sherry Wine Vinegar
½ cup – Coco Aminos or Soy Sauce
2 tbsp - Fresh Ginger, minced
2 - Garlic Cloves, minced
For the Steak:
1 ½ lb - Flank Steak
½ cup each: Rice Vinegar, Avocado Oil
1 tsp each: Ground Ginger, Garlic Powder, Salt
¼ cup - Sugar
For the Salad:
1 head - Green Cabbage, shredded
1 cup - Carrots, shredded
4 – Scallions, sliced
1 cup - Cilantro, chopped
1 tbsp each: Black Sesame Seeds, White Sesame Seeds
½ cup - Almonds, sliced
¾ cup - Ginger Sesame Dressing
Handful of Crispy Ginger Wonton Strips (optional)

1:
Prepare all of the ingredients. Preheat grill or grill pan
to medium-high heat.
2:
Mix the steak ingredients together in a bowl and let sit for 30 minutes . Then place
on grill and cook for 7 minutes on each side. Remove from grill and let rest for 10
minutes before slicing.
3:
In a large stock pot over medium-high heat, add broth, sherry vinegar, rice
vinegar, ginger, garlic, soy sauce and fish sauce. Once the broth is at a rolling boil,
add the noodles and reduce the heat to medium. After 10 minutes, add 1 cup of
carrots and half of the scallions. Cook another 10 minutes on medium.
4:
In a saucepan, bring water to a rolling boil. Place eggs in water and cook for 8
minutes. Immediately remove to an ice bath (a large bowl with ice cubes and cold
water). Let sit for 3 minutes then peel the shells.
5:
In a large salad bowl, mix together all of the salad ingredients.

Plating notes: In a shallow bowl, place a helping of the noodles in the center. Ladle
the broth over the top and sprinkle with green onions. Place a clump of shredded
carrot, and a clump of snap peas to one side of the bowl. Slice the steak on the
diagonal and lay over the top. Cut an egg in half, lengthwise, and place to one side.
Garnish with sesame seeds, if desired. Serve the salad in a separate bowl.

RICOTTA GRILLED CHEESE W/ TOMATO SOUP

Serves: 6   Prep Time: 10 min   Cook Time: 35 min

For Grilled Cheese:
12 – Sourdough Bread, thick sliced
2 cups – Ricotta Cheese
½ cup – Mozzarella Cheese, shredded
½ cup – Parmesan Cheese, shredded
½ cup – Butter
1 cup – Fresh Spinach, cut into ribbons
2 tsp each: Garlic Powder, Oregano, Parsley

For the Tomato Soup:
2 lb – Roma Tomatoes, quartered
2 tbsp – Avocado Oil
3 – Garlic Cloves, minced
½ - White Onion, diced
½ cup – Fresh Basil
1 tsp each: Salt, Pepper, Parsley

1:
Prepare all of the ingredients Preheat Panini Press or griddle to High.
2:
In a large stock pot over medium-high heat, add oil, onion, and
garlic and cook for 3 minutes. The add all of the tomatoes and
soup seasonings, stir often for 5 minutes. Reduce heat to
medium and allow to simmer stirring occasionally for 15 minutes.
3:
In a large mixing bowl, combine the cheeses, spinach, and 1 tsp each
of garlic, oregano, and parsley. Melt the butter and add 1 tsp each of
garlic powder, oregano, and parsley. Brush the melted butter on to
one side of each slice of bread. Spread a layer cheese mixture on to
half of the slices of bread (opposite the butter) and top with the
remaining bread. Begin to grill the sandwiches, approximate 4
minutes on each side for a griddle or 6 minutes total in a panini press.
4:
Add the fresh basil leaves to the soup and allow to cook another 5
minutes. Remove the soup from the stove (transfer to mixing bowl if
pot cannot be used for blending) and puree the soup with an
immersion blender.

Plating Notes: In a shallow bowl, ladle the soup in, top with some
shredded Parmesan, if desired. Diagonal cut a sandwich and serve
a on small plate.

Variations: For a creamier soup, stir in 1 cup of heavy cream after
blending soup and allow to cook for 3 minutes more.

PIZZA SALAD

Serves: 6   Prep Time: 20 Min   Cook Time: 0 Min

1 cup – Pepperoni Slices, quartered
1 cup – Canadian Bacon, cut into ½-inch pieces
1 cup – Mozzarella Cheese, shredded
6 cups – Romain Hearts, chopped
1 cup – Parmesan Cheese, shredded
½ cup – Black Olives, sliced
1 cup – White Mushrooms, sliced
1 cup – Green Bell Peppers, diced
½ - Red Onion, sliced
1 cup – Croutons
2 tsp - Oregano

For the Dressing:
½ cup – Avocado Oil
½ cup – Apple Cider Vinegar
2 tbsp each: Salt, Pepper, Oregano, Basil, Red Pepper Flakes

1:
Prepare all of the ingredients.
2:
Combine dressing ingredients in a mason jar, secure with lid and shake vigorously. Refrigerate until ready to serve.
3:
In a large salad bowl, combine lettuce, cheeses, pepperoni, Canadian bacon, croutons, and half of dressing.

Plating Notes: On plate or shallow bowl, place a portion of the salad mixture in center. Then line out the desired vegetables starting at center. Drizzle with remaining dressing. Garnish with extra parmesan cheese and oregano.

CREAM OF ASPARAGUS SOUP

Serves: 4-6   Prep time: 5 min   Cook time: 25 min

2lb - Asparagus, shave bottom 2/3 of spear, cut into ½-inch pieces
4 cups – Chicken Broth
1cup - Heavy Cream
1- White Onion, diced
2 - Garlic Cloves, minced
3 tbsp - Butter
½ cup - Parmesan Cheese, shredded
1tsp each: Salt Pepper, Rosemary

1:
Prepare all of the ingredients.
2:
In large pot over medium-high heat, melt butter and add onions and garlic. Sauté for 4 minutes, then add asparagus and sauté 5 minutes more. Add chicken broth and bring to a rolling boil. Let boil 8 minutes.
3:
Transfer to a blender and blitz until smooth. Return to pot, on medium heat, and add heavy cream and seasoning. Let simmer about 5 minutes then mix in parmesan cheese.

Plating Notes: Serve in shallow bowl with a sprinkle of parmesan cheese in the center. Serve with warm French bread, if desired.

SAUSAGE & PEPPERS OVER CHEESY GRITS

Serves: 4-6   Prep Time: 10 min   Cook Time: 20 min

2 lb – Chicken Sausage, cut into 1-inch cubes
1 – Red Bell pepper, cut into 1-inch pieces
1 – Green Bell Pepper, cut into 1-inch pieces
1 – Yellow Bell Pepper, cut into 1-inch pieces
1 – White Onion, diced
2 tbsp – Avocado Oil
2 cup – Quick Grits
1 qt – Chicken Broth
2 cup – Cheddar Cheese, Shredded
1 tsp each: Salt, Pepper, Smoked Paprika

1:
Prepare all of the ingredients.
2:
In a sauté pan, over medium-high heat, add oil, and onions and allow to cook for 4 minutes, then add sausage and cook another 4 minutes. Last add the peppers and smoked paprika and cook for 4 minutes.
3:
In a saucepan over medium-high heat, bring the chicken broth to a boil. Add salt and pepper and then whisk in grits. Reduce heat to medium low and cover, let cook for 5 minutes. Remove from heat and stir in cheese until creamy.

Plating Notes: In a shallow bowl, place a portion of cheesy grits in the center. Then spoon the sausage and pepper mixture over the top. Garnish with parsley, if desired.

GINGER DUMPLING SOUP

Serves: 4-6   Prep Time: 10 min   Cook Time: 25 min

3 qt – Chicken Broth
1 tbsp – Fresh Ginger, grated
1 cup – Sweet Red Peppers, cut in ¼-in strips
1 cup – Cabbage, cut in ribbons
1 cup – Snap Peas, ends trimmed
2 lb – Frozen Dumplings (any flavor)
3 – Scallions sliced
1 tsp – Sesame Seeds

1:
Prepare all of the ingredients.
2:
In a large stock pot over medium-high heat, bring chicken broth and ginger to a boil. Add cabbage, and red peppers and cook for 4 minutes. Add snap peas and dumplings and cook for 10 more minutes.

Plating Notes: In a bowl, ladle soup in – should serve 3-5 dumplings per serving. Sprinkle with green onions and sesame seeds.

QUESADILLA EXPLOSION SALAD

Serves: 6   Prep Time: 15 min   Cook time: 20 min

For Quesadilla:
6 – Tortillas, burrito size
3 cups – Cheddar Cheese, shredded
2 cups – Chicken, cooked & shredded
1 tsp each: Salt, Cumin, Parsley, Chili Powder
Cooking spray

For Salad:
½ head – Green Cabbage, chopped
½ head – Purple Cabbage, chopped
2 – Romaine Hearts, chopped
1 – English Cucumber, sliced and halved
1 cup – Carrots, shredded
1 cup – Grape Tomatoes, halved
1 cup – Tortilla Strips (with extra for plating)
¼ cup – Sunflower seeds
½ cup – Avocado Ranch Dressing (with extra for plating)

1:
Prepare all ingredients. Preheat oven to 400deg.
2:
Combine quesadilla seasoning with cooked chicken. Spray large
baking sheet with cooking spray and make quesadillas by placing
½ cup of cheese, and ½ cup of chicken on half of tortilla and
folding over. Place second baking sheet on top of quesadillas and
weigh down with oven safe cast iron skillet. Place in oven for 20
min.
3:
In a large salad bowl, combine all salad ingredients thoroughly.

Plating Notes: Cut quesadilla into quarters. In a large shallow
bowl, place a portion of the salad mounded in the center. Place
quesadilla quarters along one edge of bowl. Drizzle salad and
quesadillas with extra dressing and sprinkle of tortilla strips.

Variations: Use ground beef or shredded pork in place of chicken.

CHICKEN & BOK CHOY RAMEN

Serves: 6   Prep Time: 10 min   Cook Time: 30 min

1 ½ lb - Chicken Thighs, boneless, skinless, cut into ½-inch cubes
1 tbsp - Avocado Oil
3 - Garlic Cloves, minced
1 tbsp – Fresh Ginger, grated
3 cups – Chicken Broth
1 cup - Water
1/3 cup - Coco Aminos or Soy Sauce
1 tbsp - Fish Sauce
1 tsp - Onion Powder
6 - Mini Sweet Bell Peppers, seeded & coined
1/2 cup - Carrots, shredded
1/2 cup - Bean Sprouts
6 - Ramen Bricks
2-3 - Baby Bok Choy, with bottoms removed
6 - Eggs
1 - Medium Jalapeno, seeded & coined (optional)

1:
Prepare all of the ingredients. Start water boiling for eggs.
2:
In a large soup pot over medium-high heat, add oil, garlic, and ginger. Cook for 3 minutes then add chicken. Stirring occasionally, cook for 5 minutes then reduce the heat to medium.
3:
Add the chicken broth, water, coco aminos, fish sauce, and onion powder. Let boil for 5 minutes, then add the bell peppers, carrots, and bean sprouts. Cook another 5 minutes and then add ramen bricks.
4:
Once water is to a rolling boil for eggs, gently put the eggs in water, cook for exactly 8 minutes and then remove to an ice bath (a bowl full of ice and cold water) then remove after 3 minutes and peel.
5:
After 5 minutes of the ramen cooking - stirring regularly to break up the bricks - add bok choy. If you are adding the Jalapeno for some heat - this is a good time. Let cook with the lid on for about 5 minutes to soften the bok choy.

Plating Notes: In a shallow bowl, start with a scoop of the noodles, meat and veggies and then ladle over the broth. Cut each egg in half (lengthwise) and serve on the edge. Sprinkle with scallions. Garnish with white and/or black Toasted Sesame Seeds, if desired.

POTATO LEEK SOUP WITH SAUSAGE

Serves: 4-6   Prep time: 10 min   Cook time: 40 min

1lb – Chicken Sausage, cut into 1-inch pieces
2 tbsp – Avocado Oil
¼ cup – Butter
3 – Garlic Cloves, minced
4 – Leeks, cut into ½-inch slices
2 qt – Chicken Broth
1lb – Yellow Potatoes, peeled, cut into 1-inch cubes
1 tsp each: Salt, Pepper, Rosemary, Thyme, Parsley
1 cup – Heavy Cream

1:
Prepare all of the ingredients.
2:
In a large pot over medium-high heat, melt butter and add garlic
and leeks. Cook for 10 minutes, stirring regularly. Add chicken
broth, potatoes, and seasonings. Bring to a boil, cover, and reduce
heat to medium. Let cook for 20 minutes.
3:
In a sauté pan over medium-high heat, add oil. Sauté sausage until
just browned and warmed through.
4:
Remove the soup from the heat. Using an immersion blender,
blend the soup to a smooth consistency. Stir in the heavy cream.
Return to medium heat for 5 minutes.

Plating Notes: In a shallow soup bowl, ladle soup into center. Place
cooked sausage in center of bowl and garnish with parsley, if
desired

THAI RICE BOWL

Serves: 4-6   Prep Time: 15 min   Cook Time: 30 min

2 lb – Chicken Breast, cut into 1-inch chunks
1 tsp each: Salt, Pepper, Ground Ginger
1 tbsp – Avocado Oil
2 cups – Long Grain Rice
1 qt – Chicken Broth
1 bunch – Cilantro, chopped, divided
1 – Thai Salsa (recipe pg. 123)
1 cup – Bean Sprouts
½ head – Red Cabbage, chopped
1 cup – Carrots, matchsticks
½ cup – Peanuts, chopped
1 15oz can – Coconut Milk, full-fat
1 cup – Peanut Butter (all-natural)
3 tbsp – Coco Aminos or Soy Sauce
2 tbsp – Seasoned Rice Vinegar
2 tbsp - Water

1:
Prepare all of the ingredients.
2:
In a pot over medium heat, combine rice, chicken broth, and half of the cilantro. Cover and let cook 15 minutes. Remove from heat and leave lid on until ready to serve.
3:
In a large sauté pan over medium-high heat, add oil, chicken, and seasonings. Cook for 15 minutes and remove from heat.
4:
In a saucepan over medium heat, combine coconut milk, peanut butter, coco aminos, vinegar, and water. Whisk until smooth. Remove from heat.

Plating Notes: In a shallow bowl start with a portion of rice and spoonful of sauce. Top with a portion of chicken, bean sprouts, cabbage, cilantro, and carrot. Drizzle with sauce. Top with salsa and chopped peanuts.

SHRIMP BURRITO BOWL

Serves: 4-6   Prep Time: 15 min   Cook Time: 25 min

2 cups – Long Grain Rice
1 qt – Chicken Broth
1 15oz can – Sweet Corn
1 15oz can – Black Beans
1 ½ lb – Medium Shrimp, raw, peeled & deveined, raw
1 cup – Cheddar Cheese, shredded
1 – Avocado, in slices
2 – Roma Tomatoes, diced
1 bunch – Cilantro, chopped - divided
1 – Jalapeno, seeded and diced
2 tsp each: Pepper, Chili Powder, Garlic Powder, Cumin, divided
1 tbsp – Avocado Oil

1:
Prepare all of the ingredients.
2:
In a pot over medium heat, mix together rice, ½ cilantro, and chicken broth. Cover and let cook for 15 minutes. Remove from heat and leave on lid until ready to serve.
3:
In a saucepan over medium-low heat, add corn, black beans and one teaspoon each of seasoning. Let simmer, stirring occasionally, until ready to plate.
4:
In a large sauté pan over medium-high heat, add oil. Mix together remaining seasoning and sprinkle over shrimp. Add shrimp to sauté pan and cook – stirring often – until just pink, then remove from heat.

Plating Notes: In a shallow bowl, start with a portion of rice, then add corn/bean mixture over half, and cheese to opposite half. Over cheese layer avocado, tomato, jalapeno. Over corn/bean mixture add shrimp. Sprinkle cilantro over top.

Variation ideas: Replace shrimp with chicken, pork, or beef, using the same seasonings and cooking techniques.

SPAGHETTI SOUP

Serves: 4-6   Prep Time: 5 min   Cook Time: 30 min

1 ½ lb – Medium Shell Pasta
2 15oz can – Tomato Puree
1 9oz can – Tomato Paste
1 cup – Parmesan Cheese, grated
1 tsp each: Salt, Pepper, Oregano, Basil, Parsley, Red Pepper Flakes

1:
Prepare all of the ingredients
2:
In a large pot, bring water to boil for pasta. Add pasta and prepare as directed on package. Drain all but 3 cups of pasta water from pot.
3:
Stir in tomato paste and puree, as well as seasonings. Reduce heat to medium and let simmer for 10 minutes. Then stir in parmesan cheese.

Variation ideas: Add mini meatballs or Italian sausage chunks to this soup when the tomato products are added.

GRILLED SALAD

Serves: 4-6   Prep Time: 25 min   Cook Time: 30 min

4 cups – Spring Mix
1 cup – Gorgonzola Cheese
4 ears – Corn, in husk
1 cup – Cherry Tomatoes, halved
1 cup – Sweet Peppers, sliced
½ cup – Fresh Parsley, coarse chopped
½ - Red Onion, sliced
1 cup – Brussel Sprouts, shaved
For Steak:
2 lb – Flank Steak
½ cup – Avocado Oil
½ cup – Apple Cider Vinegar
2 tbsp each: Salt, Paprika, Garlic Powder
For Dressing:
¼ cup – Balsamic Vinegar
½ cup – Avocado Oil
¼ cup – Dijon Mustard
2 tbsp – Worcestershire Sauce
1 – Lemon, zested & juiced

1:
Prepare all of the ingredients. Preheat grill or grill
pan to medium-high.
2:
Combine steak ingredients in a bowl and put in refrigerator for 15
minutes. Put Corn, in husk, on grill for 15 minutes
3:
In a small mixing bowl, combine dressing ingredients and put in
refrigerator until ready to serve.
4:
When steak is done marinating, put on grill and cook on each side for 8
minutes. Remove husks from corn and return to grill, cooking for
remainder for time with steak. Remove steak to cutting board and let
rest. Remove corn from cob by standing corn on end and cutting straight
down from top to bottom.
5:
Combine corn and remaining salad ingredients in a large salad bowl,
drizzle with half of dressing.

Plating Notes: Cut steak into ½-inch strips on the diagonal. Place a
serving of the salad mix on center of plate or in shallow bowl. Lay a
portion of the steak across center of salad and drizzle with dressing.
Sprinkle with additional Gorgonzola Cheese and parsley, if desired.

TURKEY BEAN CHILI

Serves: 4-6   Prep Time: 10 min   Cook Time: 30 min

2 lb – Ground Turkey
½ - Yellow Onion, diced
3 – Garlic Cloves, minced
2 tbsp – Avocado Oil
2 qt – Chicken Broth
1 15oz can – Diced Tomatoes
3 15 oz can – Red Kidney Beans, drained
4 – Celery Stalks, sliced
1 7oz can – Green Chilies
1 8oz can – Tomato Paste
1 tbsp – Corn Starch, mixed with 1 tbsp warm water
1 tsp each: Salt, Pepper, Cumin, Parsley
1 tbsp – Chili Powder
½ cup – Cheddar Cheese, shredded, for topping
1 cup – Sour Cream, for topping
3 – Scallions, sliced, for topping

1:
Prepare all of the ingredients.
2:
In a large stock pot over medium-high heat, add oil, onions, garlic, and seasonings. Cook for 3 minutes then add ground turkey. Cook until turkey is cooked through.
3:
Add chicken broth, tomatoes, beans, celery, chilies, and tomato paste. Bring to boil then cover pot and reduce heat to medium. Let cook for 20 minutes.
4:
Stir in cornstarch slurry and cook 5 more minutes to allow to thicken.

Plating Notes: In a large bowl, ladle a portion of chili into bowl. Sprinkle with cheese, then add a dollop of sour cream and finally sprinkle with scallions.

Variations: Can be made with any ground meat.

ORANGE CHICKEN SALAD

Serves: 4-6   Prep Time: 20 min   Cook Time: 10 min

4 cups – Spring Mix
2 cups – Fresh Spinach
1 cup – Red Cabbage, shredded
4 – Scallions, sliced
1 – English Cucumber, cut into ¼-inch slices
1 cup – Carrots, matchsticks
1 cup – Mandarin Orange segments, drained
½ cup – Almonds, slivers

For the Chicken:
1 lb – Chicken Breast, cut into ½-inch chunks
1 tbsp – Avocado Oil
1 tbsp – Orange Juice (no sugar added)
1 tbsp – Coco Aminos or Soy Sauce
1 tsp each: Salt, Ground Ginger, Garlic Powder, Parsley

For the Dressing:
½ cup – Orange Juice (no sugar added)
¼ cup – Avocado Oil
1 tbsp – Rice Wine Vinegar
1 tbsp – Fresh Ginger, grated
2 tsp – Dijon Mustard
2 tsp – Honey
1 tsp each: Salt, Pepper, Sesame Seeds

1:
Prepare all of the ingredients.
2:
Combine dressing ingredients in a small bowl and refrigerator
until ready to serve.
3:
In a bowl, combine ingredients for chicken. In a large sauté pan
over medium-high heat, add chicken, and stir frequently for
10 minutes. Remove from heat and let cool.
4:
In a large salad bowl, combine all vegetables and almonds with
half of prepared dressing.

Plating Notes: On a plate, place a portion of the salad mixture and
top with a portion of the cooled chicken. Drizzle with remaining
dressing and garnish with sesame seeds, if desired.

WHITE BEAN CHICKEN SOUP

Serves: 4-6   Prep Time: 10 min   Cook Time: 35 min

1 ½ lb – Chicken Breast, cut into ½-inch chunks
½ - Red Onion, diced
3 – Garlic cloves, minced
2 tbsp – Avocado Oil
2 tbsp – Butter
2 tbsp – Flour (AP or Wheat)
4 – Celery Stalks, sliced
3 15oz cans – Cannelloni Beans, drained
1 7oz can – Green Chilies
2 qt – Chicken Broth
1 tsp each: Salt, Pepper, Parsley 1 tbsp – Chili
Powder

1:
Prepare all of the ingredients.
2:
In a large stock pot over medium-high heat, add oil, onions, garlic,
and seasonings. Cook for 3 minutes then add chicken and cook
until no longer pink.
3:
Move chicken to one side of pot and add butter. Once melted, add
flour, and mix with butter. Let cook for 3 minutes then stir in with
chicken. Add chicken broth, green chilies, beans, and celery. Bring
to boil, then reduce heat to medium, cover and cook for 20
minutes. Remove lid and cook additional 5 minutes, stirring
occasionally.

CHOPPED COBB SALAD

Serves: 4-6   Prep time: 20 min   Cook time: 10min

6 cups – Romaine Hearts, chopped
2 cups – Red Cabbage, shredded
1 cup – Sharp Cheddar Cheese, shredded
1 cup – Swiss Cheese, shredded
1 lb – Bacon, cut in ½-inch pieces
1 lb – Turkey Deli Meat (unsliced), cut in ½-inch cubes
1 lb – Ham steak, cut in ½-inch cubes
1 cup – Grape Tomatoes, halved
1 – English Cucumber, cut in ¼-in slices
1 cup – Carrots, matchsticks
4 – Eggs, hard-boiled, diced
½ cup – Sunflower Seeds, shelled

For Dressing:
1 cup – Bleu Cheese, crumbled
½ cup – Avocado Mayo
½ cup – Greek Yogurt
½ cup – Heavy Cream
1 tbsp – Lemon Juice
½ tbsp – Worchester Sauce
1 tsp each: Salt, Pepper, Garlic Powder Parsley

1:
Prepare all of the ingredients.
2:
Combine dressing ingredients in a bowl. Cover and place in refrigerator until ready to serve.
3:
In a frying pan over medium-high heat, cook bacon until crispy. Remove to paper towel to drain excess oil.
4:
In a large salad bowl, combine romaine, cabbage, and carrots. Portion lettuce mixture on to plates. Line up toppings (meats, cheeses, veggies). Drizzle dressing over top and sprinkle with sunflower seeds.

SAUSAGE & VEGGIE RICE BOWL

Serves: 4-6   Prep Time: 15 Min   Cook Time: 20 min

2 lb – Chicken Sausage, any flavor, cut into ½-inch slices
1 – Buttered Rice (recipe pg. 124)
2 cups – Broccoli, chopped
2 cups – Zucchini, chopped
1 – Red Onion, diced
1 – Garlic Clove, minced
1 – Red Bell Pepper, chopped
3 tbsp – Avocado Oil
2 tbsp – Lemon Juice
1 tsp each: Salt, Red Pepper Flakes, Oregano

1:
Prepare all of the ingredients.
2:
In a large sauté pan over medium-high heat, add 1 tablespoon of oil and sausage. Cook for 8 minutes then remove sausage from pan. Add remaining oil to pan.
3:
Add onion and garlic to pan and cook for 3 minutes. Then add broccoli, zucchini, bell pepper, lemon juice and seasonings. Cook another 8 minutes.

Plating Notes: In a shallow bowl, place a portion of rice. Lay a portion of sausage down center of bowl. Place a portion of the vegetable mixture to one side of the sausage.

HEALTHIER FARE

BAKED SHRIMP "BOIL"

Serves: 4   Prep Time: 5 min   Cook Time: 40 min

2 lb - Medium Shrimp, shell-off, tail-off
1 lb - Baby Red Potatoes, quartered
1 lb - Chicken Andouille Sausage, cut into 1-inch pieces
4 ears - Corn, split in half
1 - Yellow Onion, sliced
2 tbsp - Avocado Oil
1 tsp each: Salt, Pepper, Garlic Powder, Red Pepper Flake, Paprika,
Parsley, Thyme

1:
Prepare all of the ingredients. Preheat the oven to 400F.
2:
Brush sheet pan with 1 tablespoon oil. Put potatoes and corn on
the pan and put into oven for 20 minutes
3:
In a bowl, mix shrimp, sausage, remaining avocado oil, garlic,
onion and seasonings. Remove the potatoes & corn from the
oven, add the shrimp & sausage mixture to the pan and
incorporate. Then put the pan back into the oven for another 20
minutes.

Plating Notes: Each plate should get at least 1 piece of corn. Serve
a portion of the Shrimp "Boil" onto a plate or shallow bowl and
garnish with parsley.

Side Dish Suggestion: Buttered Rice (recipe pg. 124) or Pasta Salad
(recipe pg. 126)

GREEN CHILI CHICKEN LASAGNA

Serves: 4-6   Prep Time: 15 min   Cook Time: 45 min

2 lb – Chicken Breast, each cut in 3 large chunks
1 qt – Chicken Broth
1 lb – Lasagna Noodles, oven ready
1 cup – Greek Yogurt
1 7oz can – Green Chilies
1 tsp each: Salt, Pepper, Cumin, Chili Powder
1 cup – Ricotta Cheese
2 cup – Cheddar Cheese, finely shredded

For the Salsa Verde:
6 – Tomatillos, diced
3 – Garlic Cloves, minced
½ - White Onion, diced
½ - Jalapeno, seeded and diced
1 tbsp – Avocado Oil
1 tsp – Salt

1:
Prepare all of the ingredient. Preheat oven to 400deg.
2:
In a large pot over medium-high heat, add chicken broth, 2 cups of water and chicken. Let cook for 15 minutes. Then remove chicken from pot and shred.
3:
In a bowl, combine ingredients for Salsa Verde and blitz with immersion blender until smooth.
4:
In another bowl combine green chilies, yogurt, ricotta, 1 cup of cheddar cheese and seasonings.
5:
In a 13x9 baking dish layer as follows: Salsa Verde, lasagna noodles, ricotta mixture, chicken, Salsa Verde and so on for 3 full layers, then sprinkle with remaining cheddar cheese and put in oven for 30 minutes.

Variation: Use shredded Pork in place of chicken.

EGG & CORN SALAD WRAPS

Serves: 6   Prep Time: 15 min   Cook Time: 15 min

10 – Eggs
2 15oz cans – Sweet Corn, drained
4 – Scallions, sliced
1 – English Cucumber, diced
1 cup – Greek Yogurt
2 – Garlic Cloves, minced
2 cups – Alfalfa Sprouts
6 – Tortillas, burrito sized (tomato or spinach flavor is suggested)
1 tsp each: Salt, Pepper, Basil, Ground Ginger

1:
Prepare all of the ingredients. Begin boiling water.
2:
Once the water is boiling, gently place eggs into water and let cook for 10 minutes. Remove to ice bath (ice and cold water in a large bowl) and let sit for 3 minutes before removing. Peel each egg and dice.
3:
In a large bowl, combine corn, scallions, cucumber, garlic, seasonings, and yogurt. Fold in egg.
4:
Place tortilla flat and add a portion of egg salad in center. Top with alfalfa sprouts and wrap tortilla.

Side Dish Suggestion: Cucumber Salad (recipe pg. 118)

PHILLY CHEESE STEAK STUFFED PEPPERS

Serves: 4-6   Prep Time: 10 min   Cook Time: 40 min

2 lb - Ground Beef
1 - small Red Onion, diced
1 cup - White Mushrooms, sliced
3 - Garlic Cloves, minced
1 tsp - Avocado Oil
16 - Provolone Cheese Slices
4 - large Bell Peppers (any color), halved, seeded
1 tsp each: Salt, Pepper, Basil, Red Pepper Flakes

1:
Prepare all of the ingredients. Preheat oven to 400deg.
2:
In a large sauté pan over medium-high heat, add oil, garlic, and onion, and cook for 3 minutes. Add ground beef and seasonings and cook for 8 minutes. Then add the mushrooms for 8 minutes more
3:
On a baking sheet, place the bell pepper halves, open side up. First put a slice of the provolone in the bottom of the pepper. Fill with mushroom & meat mixture. Then put another slice of provolone on top of each cup. Bake for 20 minutes.

Side Dish Suggestions: Whipped Garlic Cauliflower (recipe pg. 112) or Street Corn (recipe pg. 121)

HONEY MUSTARD CHICKEN

Serves: 4-6   Prep Time: 30 min   Cook Time: 45 min

1 ½ lb – Chicken Thighs, boneless, skinless
½ cup – Yellow Mustard
¼ cup – Honey
¼ cup – Avocado Oil
¼ cup – Apple Cider Vinegar
1 tsp each: Salt, Pepper, Garlic Powder, Onion Powder, Parsley.

1:
Prepare all of the ingredients. Preheat oven to 400deg.
2:
In a mixing bowl, combine all ingredient and let sit at least 20 min.
3:
Put chicken on a cooking rack on a baking sheet and brush with remaining marinade. Put in oven for 25 minutes.

Side Dish Suggestion: Roasted Potatoes & Cauliflower (recipe pg. 120) or Potato Salad (recipe pg. 125)

CHICKEN SALAD SANDWICHES

Serves: 6   Prep Time: 10 min   Cook Time: 15 min

12 slices – Sourdough Bread
1 ½ lb – Chicken Thighs, boneless, skinless
½ - Red Onion, diced
1 cup – Sweet Peppers, seeded, cut into ½-in pieces
1 cup – Celery, cut into ½-in pieces
½ cup – Avocado Mayo
¼ cup – Avocado Oil
¼ cup – Apple Cider Vinegar
1 tbsp – Lemon Juice
1 tsp each: Salt, Pepper, Garlic Powder, Oregano, Basil

1:
Prepare all of the ingredients.
2:
In a large pot, bring 4 cups of water to boil. Add chicken thighs and cook for 15 minutes. Room from water and shred and let cool for at least 10 minutes (Can also use Rotisserie Chicken instead).
3:
In a mixing bowl combine remaining ingredients, minus the bread. Once the chicken is cool, mix it in with the other ingredients
4:
Toast the bread, either in toaster or on a baking sheet for 8 minutes in a 400deg oven.

Plating Notes: Place one piece of bread on a plate. Put ½ cup of the chicken salad on the bread, top with second piece of bread. Use two toothpicks through sandwich to help hold it together and cut on the diagonal

Side Dish Suggestion: Cucumber Salad (recipe pg. 118) or Corn Salad (recipe pg. 117)

SUMMER VEGGIE SKILLET

Serves: 4-6   Prep Time: 15 Min   Cook Time: 40 Min

1 ½ lb – Sweet Potatoes, peeled & cut into ½-inch chunks
½ - Yellow Onion, diced
2 – Garlic Cloves, Minced
2 15oz can – Black Beans, rinsed & drained
1 ½ lb – Ground Turkey
1 – Zucchini, diced
4 – Corn Ears, kernels removed
2 tbsp – Avocado Oil
1 tsp each: Salt, Pepper, Parsley, Cayenne
1 cup – Sour Cream
½ cup – Balsamic Vinegar

1:
Prepare all of the ingredients.
2:
In a large sauté pan over medium-high heat, add 1 tbsp oil,
onions, and garlic. Let cook for 3 minutes then add turkey and
seasonings. Cook for 10 minutes and remove from pan.
3:
Add remaining oil, potatoes and zucchini. Cook for 5 minutes.
Reduce heat to medium and return turkey to pan. Add corn and
beans and mix thoroughly. Cover and cook for 20 minutes.
4:
In a small bowl, combine sour cream and balsamic vinegar.

Plating Notes: In a shallow bowl, place a portion of skillet. Drizzle
with Balsamic sour cream and garnish with parsley, if desired.

SPICY GARLIC PARMESAN WINGS

Serves: 4-6   Prep Time: 10 min   Cook Time: 35 min

3 lb – Chicken Wings, separated into wing & drumettes
½ lb – Butter, melted
2 – Garlic Cloves, minced
½ cup – Parmesan Cheese, shredded
1 tsp – Red Pepper Flakes
1 tbsp – Avocado Oil

1:
Prepare all of the ingredient. Preheat oven to 425deg.
2:
In a large bowl, toss chicken wings with avocado oil until well coated. Place wings on baking sheet. Place on lower rack of oven for 30 minutes. Wash large bowl.
3:
In a small dish, combine remaining chicken ingredients. Remove chicken wings from oven and return to (cleaned) large bowl. Pour melted butter mixture over wings and toss until well coated. Return to oven for 5 minutes more.

Side Dish Suggestion: Baked Cauliflower (recipe pg. 122) or Potato Salad (recipe pg. 125)

Variation: Omit Red Pepper Flakes and replace with Italian seasoning for non-spicy wings.

INDIVIDUAL CHAFFLE MEAT-LOVERS PIZZA

Serves: 1   Prep Time: 5 min   Cook Time: 20 min

For Chaffle:
1 – Egg, beaten
½ cup – Mozzarella Cheese, shredded
½ cup – Cheddar Cheese, shredded
½ tsp each: Garlic Powder, Oregano

Pizza Topping:
¼ cup – Pizza Sauce
4 slices – Pepperoni, cut in half
2 slices – Canadian Bacon, cut in quarters
1 tbsp – Bacon Crumbles
¼ cup – Mozzarella Cheese, shredded
½ tsp – Oregano

1:
Prepare all of the ingredients. Preheat oven to 425deg. Preheat waffle maker to high.
2:
In a bowl, mix the egg and chaffle seasonings together, then add the cheese. Pour into waffle maker and spread out evenly. Depending on the waffle maker, cook for 4-6 min.
3:
On a baking sheet, build the pizza starting with a chaffle, spread with pizza sauce, ¾ of the cheese, meat toppings, then remaining cheese and sprinkle with oregano. Bake for 8-10 minutes.

Variation: Any toppings will work for these individual pizzas.

SALSA CHICKEN

Serves: 4-6   Prep Time: 15 min   Cook Time: 30 min

2 lb – Chicken Breast, cut into 1-inch chunks
2 tbsp – Avocado Oil
4 – Roma Tomatoes, diced
1 – Red Onion, diced
1 – Jalapeno, seeded & diced
3 – Garlic Cloves, minced
1 cup – Fresh Cilantro, chopped
2 tbsp – Lime Juice
2 cups – Mozzarella Cheese
1 tsp each: Salt, Cumin, Chili Powder
1 cup – Avocado, sliced

1:
Prepare all of the ingredients. Preheat oven to 400 deg.
2:
Brush the bottom and sides of a 13x9 baking dish with oil. Place chicken in single layer, covering bottom of pan. Sprinkle with seasonings.
3:
In a bowl, combine the tomatoes, red onion, jalapeno, garlic, half of the cilantro, and lemon juice. Layer the salsa on top of chicken. Then sprinkle mozzarella on top of the salsa and top with half of the remaining cilantro. Put into oven and bake for 30 minutes.

Plating Notes: Serve on plate with fresh avocado and garnish with remaining cilantro.

Side Dish Suggestions: Buttered Rice (recipe pg. 124) or Rice & Beans (recipe pg. 129)

SWEET POTATO SKILLET

Serves: 4-6   Prep Time: 15 Min   Cook Time: 30 Min

4 – Sweet Potatoes, peeled, cut into ½-inch pieces
2 tbsp – Avocado Oil
2 lb – Chicken Sausage, cut into 1-inch pieces
½ - White Onion, diced
2 – Garlic Cloves
1 ½ cup – Mozzarella Cheese, shredded
1 tsp each: Salt, Pepper, Red Pepper Flakes, Parsley

1:
Prepare all of the ingredients.
2:
In a large skillet or sauté pan over medium-high heat, add 1 tbsp oil. Add potatoes to pan and let cook for 10 minutes while stirring only occasionally. Push potatoes to one side of pan and remaining oil, onions, and garlic. Cook for 3 minutes then add sausage and seasonings. Cook for 5 minutes. Combine with potatoes, cover pan, and cook for 10 more minutes.
3:
Remove cover and sprinkle cheese over top of sausage and sweet potato mixture. Replace cover and cook another 5 minutes, until cheese is melted.

Plating Notes: In a shallow bowl, place portion of skillet and garnish with Parsley.

CHICKEN BURGERS

Serves: 6   Prep Time: 15 Min   Cook Time: 15 Min

2 lb – Ground Chicken
1 tbsp – Avocado Oil
2 – Eggs, beaten
1 cup – Gorgonzola Cheese, crumbled
2 – Garlic Cloves, Minced
1 tbsp – Lemon Juice
2 tsp each: Salt, Pepper, Smoked Paprika, Dill 1 head – Green
Leaf Lettuce, for topping
2 – Beefsteak Tomatoes, sliced, for topping
1 – Red Onion, Sliced, for topping
6 – Brioche Buns
¼ cup – Butter, melted
1 cup – Sour Cream
½ cup – Balsamic Vinaigrette

1:
Prepare all of the Ingredients. Preheat grill or grill pan to medium-
high. Preheat oven to 450deg.
2:
In a large bowl, combine chicken, oil, cheese, egg, garlic, lemon
juice and seasonings. Form into six ¾-in thick patties,
approximately 3 inches in diameter. Place patties on grill and
cook for 7 minutes on each side.
3:
In a small bowl combine sour cream and balsamic vinaigrette.
4:
Brush buns with melted butter and place (butter up) on a baking
sheet and place in oven for 8 minutes.
5:
On a bun, place on chicken burger and a dollop of Balsamic Sour
Cream, then top with desired veggies.

Side Dish Suggestion: Greek Cucumber Salad (recipe pg. 118) or
Street Corn (recipe pg. 121)

GARLIC CHICKEN & BROCCOLI BITES

Serves: 4-6   Prep Time: 10 min   Cook Time: 25 min

1 ½ lb – Chicken Breast, cut into 1-inch chunks
3 cups – Broccoli, cut into 1-inch chunks
3 tbsp – Avocado Oil
4 – Garlic Cloves, minced
1 tbsp – Lemon Juice
1 tsp each: Salt, Pepper, Parsley, Red Pepper Flakes

1:
Prepare all of the ingredients. Preheat oven to 400deg.
2:
On a large cooking sheet, thoroughly combine all ingredients and
flatten out to a single layer. Place on top rack of oven and bake for
25 minutes.

Variations: Use Steak instead of Chicken, and reduce cook time to
15 minutes

Side Dish Suggestion: Pasta in Red Sauce (recipe pg. 128)

SWEET POTATO & SAUSAGE HASH

Serves 4-6   Prep Time: 10 min   Cook Time: 30 min

2 lb - Sweet Potato, peeled and cubed
2 lb - Smoked Sausage, cubed
1 - Yellow Bell Pepper, cut into 1-inch pieces
1 - Orange Bell Pepper, cut into 1-inch pieces
½ - Red Onion, diced
1 cup - Fresh Spinach
3 tbsp - Avocado Oil
1 tsp each: Salt, Pepper, Paprika, Ground Mustard, Celery Seed, Cayenne, Nutmeg
4 — Eggs, fried

1:
Prepare all of the ingredients.
2:
In a large sauté pan over medium-high heat, add 1 tablespoon of oil, half of seasonings and sweet potatoes. Cook, stirring occasionally, for 8 minutes. Add the Red Onion and continue cooking for 5 minutes, then add the Bell Peppers and cook for 5 minutes. Remove from pan and set aside.
3:
In a separate frying pan over medium-high heat, add 1 tablespoon of oil and begin frying eggs. (Over medium is suggested, but cook to desired doneness.)
4:
In the sauté pan, add the remaining oil, sausage, and remaining seasonings. Pan fry for 8 minutes.

Plating Notes: Place a spoonful of the hash mixture, and a spoonful of the Smoked Sausage in a shallow bowl or flat plate. Place a small layer of fresh Spinach over the top. Then gentle place a fried egg on top. Garnish with parsley, if desired.

TURKEY RICE & BEANS

Serves: 4-6   Prep Time: 10 min   Cook Time: 30 min

1 ½ lb – Ground Turkey
3 tbsp – Avocado Oil
1 tsp each: Salt, Paprika, Cumin, Parsley
½ - Yellow Onion, diced
3 – Garlic Cloves, minced
1 – Green Bell Pepper, cut in ½-inch pieces
1 – Red Bell Pepper, cut in ½-inch pieces
1 15oz can – Tomato Puree
2 cups – Long Grain Rice
1 qt – Chicken Broth
2 15oz can – Red Kidney Beans, drained

1:
Prepare all of the ingredients.
2:
In a large sauté pan over medium-high heat, add 1 tbsp oil, onions, and garlic. Cook for 3 minutes then add ground turkey, bell peppers, and seasonings. Cook for 8 minutes and remove from pan.
3:
In same pan, add remaining oil and rice. Sauté for 3 minutes then add tomato puree, chicken broth, beans, and meat mixture. Bring just to boil, reduce heat to medium and cover pan. Cook for 15 minutes.

ONE POT CAJUN CHICKEN ALFREDO

Serves: 4-6   Prep Time: 10 min   Cook Time: 45 min

1 ½ lb – Chicken Breast, cut in 1-inchch chunks
1 lb – Chicken Sausage, Andouille Flavor, cut in 1-inchch chunks
1 ½ lb – Short Pasta (penne, rotini, medium shells)
3 tbsp – Avocado Oil
3 – Garlic Cloves, minced
1 qt – Chicken Broth
2 cups – Heavy Cream
1 cup – Parmesan Cheese, shredded
1 cup – Parsley, chopped
1 tsp each: Salt, Pepper, Red Pepper Flakes, Garlic Powder, Onion Powder
½ tsp – Cayenne

1:
Prepare all of the ingredients.
2:
In a large stock pot over medium-high heat, add oil and garlic. Cook for 3 minutes then add chicken pieces, cayenne, and seasonings. Cook for 5 minutes and then add sausage. Cook an additional 5 minutes.
3:
Add pasta and chicken broth. Bring just to a boil, reduce heat to medium low and cover. Cook for 15 minutes. Remove cover and stir in parsley, heavy cream, and parmesan cheese. Cook for 5 minutes more

SWEET PEPPER NACHOS

Serves: 4-6   Prep Time: 20 min   Cook Time: 25 min

1 ½ lb – Ground Turkey
1 tbsp – Avocado Oil
1 tsp each: Salt, Chili Powder, Cumin, Garlic Powder 2 lb
– Sweet Peppers, seeded, halved lengthwise
½ - Red Onion, diced
1 15oz can – Black Beans, drained
1 15oz can – Sweet Corn, drained
1 cup – Cheddar Cheese, finely shredded

For Topping:
1 – Restaurant-style Salsa (recipe pg. 123)
1 cup – Sour Cream
½ cup – Cilantro, chopped
1 cup – Pickled Jalapenos

1:
Prepare all of the ingredients. Preheat oven to 425deg
2:
In a large sauté pan over medium-high heat, add oil, ground
turkey, and seasoning, and cook for 8 minutes.
3:
In a small bowl combine onion, black beans, and corn.
4:
On a large baking sheet, arrange sweet pepper halves with the
opening up. In each pepper put a spoon of cooked turkey, top with
bean mixture, then with cheese. Place in oven and bake for 10
minutes. Top with desired toppings before serving.

Side Dish Suggestion: Rice & Beans (recipe pg. 129)

CHICKEN & MUSHROOM LETTUCE WRAPS

Serves: 4-6   Prep Time: 15 min   Cook Time: 15 min

2 lb – Chicken thighs, boneless, skinless, cut into ½-inch pieces
1 lb – White Mushrooms, diced
½ - White Onion, diced
4 – Garlic Cloves, minced
4 – Scallions, sliced
1 cup – Carrot, matchsticks
2 tbsp – Fresh Ginger, grated
2 tbsp – Avocado Oil
2 tbsp – Coco Aminos or Soy Sauce
1 tbsp – Sriracha
1 tsp each: Salt, Pepper, Sesame Seeds
1 head – Butter Leaf Lettuce

1:
Prepare all of the ingredients.
2:
In a large sauté pan over medium-high heat, add oil and onions.
Let cook for 2 minutes then add chicken and mushrooms. Cook
for 5 minutes.
3:
In a small bowl, combine garlic, ginger, coco aminos, sriracha and
seasonings and add mixture to sauté pan. Cook, stirring
frequently, for 10 minutes. Add one half of scallions and carrots
and cook for 5 minutes more.

Plating Notes: Place 2-3 lettuce leaves on a plate and fill each with
a portion of the chicken mixture. Sprinkle with remaining
scallions, garnish with sesame seeds if desired.

Side Dish Suggestions: Garlic Noodles (recipe pg. 119) or Buttered
Rice (recipe pg. 124)

TURKEY PATTY MELTS

Serves: 6   Prep Time: 15 min   Cook Time: 25 min

For Patties:
2 lb – Ground Turkey
½ - White Onion, finely diced
2 – Garlic Cloves, minced
2 – Eggs, beaten
1 cup – Panko Crumbs
2 tbsp – Lemon Juice
2 tsp each: Salt, Pepper, Dill, Paprika, Parsley

6 – Swiss Cheese Slices

For Bread:
12 – Sourdough Slices
¼ cup – Butter, melted
½ tsp each: Garlic Powder, Parsley

For Spread:
½ cup – Avocado Mayo
½ cup – Dijon Mustard
¼ cup – Worchester Sauce
1 tsp each: Salt, Parsley, Garlic Powder, Red Pepper Flakes

1:
Prepare all of the ingredients. Preheat Panini Press to high.
2:
In a bowl, combine ingredients for patties and form into six 4-inch diameter
– ½-inch thick patties. In a large sauté pan over medium-high heat, cook
turkey patties for 4 minutes on each side. Remove from pan.
3:
Combine ingredients for spread and set aside.
4:
Combine melted butter with garlic powder and parsley. Brush onto one
side of each piece of bread. Brush spread on to opposite side of each
piece of bread. Build sandwich as follows (from the counter up) buttered
side of bread, spread side of bread, turkey patty, swiss cheese, spread
side of bread, buttered side of bread. Make remaining sandwiches.
5:
Place sandwich in Panini Press until cheese is melted and bread is golden
brown – about 6 minutes.

Side Dish Suggestions: Honey Roasted Carrots (recipe pg. 127) or Corn
Salad (recipe pg. 117)

SLOPPY JOE STUFFED SWEET POTATOES

Serves: 4-6   Prep Time: 10 min   Cook Time: 60 min

6 – Large Sweet Potatoes
1 ½ lb – Ground Turkey
3 – Garlic Cloves, minced
½ - White Onion, diced
1 tbsp – Avocado Oil
1 – Green Bell Pepper, diced
1 15oz can – Tomato Puree
1 cup – Chicken Broth
¼ cup – Butter
½ cup – Heavy Cream
1 cup – Mozzarella Cheese
1 tsp each: Salt, Pepper, Chili Powder, Cumin, Oregano

1:
Prepare all of the ingredients. Preheat oven to 400deg.
2:
Place sweet potatoes on baking sheet and place in oven for 40 minutes.
3:
In a large sauté pan over medium-high heat, add oil, onions, and garlic. Let cook for 3 minutes then add green bell peppers and cook 3 minutes longer. Next add ground turkey and seasonings. Once turkey is thoroughly cooked through, add tomato puree and chicken broth. Reduce heat to medium low and continue to cook for 15 minutes, stirring occasionally.
4:
Remove potatoes from oven and let cool 5 minutes. Remove a cap horizontally, and scoop potatoes into a bowl. Add heavy cream and butter to potatoes and mix thoroughly. Add sloppy joe mixture to potato mixture and mix well. Evenly divide the mixture into the potato shells. Sprinkle with mozzarella cheese and return to oven for 10 minutes.

Side Dish Suggestion: Cucumber Salad (recipe pg. 118) or Baked Cauliflower (recipe pg. 122)

SIDE DISHES

& SAUCES

WHIPPED GARLIC CAULIFLOWER

Serves: 4-6   Prep Time: 5 min   Cook Time: 15 min

2 – Cauliflower Heads, cut into flowerets
3 - Garlic Cloves, minced
½ cup – Butter, melted
½ cup - Heavy Cream
1 tsp each: Salt, White Pepper
Parsley for Garnishing

1:
Prepare all of the ingredients. Start large pot of boiling water.
2:
Put the cauliflower into the boiling water. Let cook for 15 minutes. Drain in a strainer and transfer to a large bowl. Add the melted butter, garlic, and seasonings and use an immersion blender to break up the cauliflower. Then add the heavy cream and blend until the mixture is a creamy consistency.

GARLIC PARMESAN RICE

Serves: 4-6   Prep Time: 5 min   Cook Time: 25 min

2 cup – Long-grain Rice
1 qt – Chicken Broth
3 – Garlic Cloves, minced
½ cup – White Wine
¾ cup – Parmesan Cheese, shredded
½ cup – Heavy Cream
1 tsp each: Salt, Red Pepper Flakes, Oregano
2 tsp – Parsley

1:
Prepare all of the ingredients.
2:
In a large pot over medium-high heat, add butter and garlic. Add white wine while stirring constantly for 3 minutes. Add seasonings and rice to pan and stir often, for 3 minutes. Then add the broth, cover pan, and reduce to medium heat. Allow to cook 20 minutes.
3:
Remove lid and stir in heavy cream, parsley, and parmesan. Return lid and cook 5 minutes more.

POTATO STACKS

Serves: 4-6   Prep Time: 10 min   Cook Time: 35
                            min

1 lb – Golden Potatoes, sliced ¼-inch pieces
2 tbsp – Avocado Oil
1 tsp each: Salt, Pepper, Dill, Garlic Powder

1:
Prepare all of the ingredients. Preheat oven to 425deg
2:
In a bowl, mix potato ingredients thoroughly. In a muffin tin, stack
each space with potatoes. Put in oven to bake for 35 min.

POTATOES AU GRATIN

Serves: 4-6   Prep Time: 15 min   Cook Time: 35 min

2 lb – Red Potatoes, peeled & cut into ½-in slices
3 tbsp – Butter
3 tbsp – Flour (AP or Whole Wheat)
2 cups – Chicken Broth
1 cup – Heavy Cream
2 cups – Cheddar Cheese, shredded, divided
1 ½ cups – Parmesan Cheese, shredded, divided
1 tsp each: Garlic Salt, Parsley

1:
Prepare all of the ingredients. Preheat oven to 425deg.
2:
In a saucepan over medium heat, melt butter and add garlic salt. Whisk in flour and let cook for 3 minutes. Whisk in chicken broth and cook for 2 minutes. Whisk in Heavy Cream and cook 2 minutes. Whisk in 1 ½ cup Cheddar and 1 cup Parmesan Cheese and cook 2 minutes.
3:
In a 13x9 baking dish, fill with sliced potatoes. Pour cheese sauce over top and stir together to evenly coat. Top with remaining cheese and parsley. Place in oven for 35 minutes

TZATZIKI SAUCE

Serves 4-6   Prep Time: 15 min

16 oz – Greek Yogurt
1 – Cucumber, peeled, seeded, grated, drained
2 – Garlic Cloves, minced
1 tbsp – Lemon Juice
1 tsp each: Salt, Dill, Pepper

1:
Prepare all ingredients.
2:
In a mixing bowl, combine Tzatziki Sauce ingredients. Place in refrigerator until ready to serve. (up to 3 days)

CORN SALAD

Serves: 4-6   Prep Time: 5 min   Cook Time: 10 min

1lb – Bacon, cut into ½-inch pieces
2 15oz cans – Sweet Corn, drained
½ cup – Mayo
½ cup – Parmesan Cheese, grated
¼ cup – Fresh Parsley, chopped
2 – Garlic Cloves, minced
¼ - Red Onion, diced
1 tsp each: Salt, Pepper, Paprika

1:
Prepare all of the ingredients.
2:
In a large frying pan over medium-high, add bacon. Cook until desired crispiness. Removed to plate covered with paper towel and let cool at least 5 minutes.
3:
In a large mixing bowl, combine all ingredients (included cooled bacon).

CUCUMBER SALAD 4 WAYS

Serves: 4-6   Prep Time: 15min

4 – Cucumbers
1 – Red Onion, diced

Basic Vinaigrette:
¼ cup - Apple Cider Vinegar
½ cup – Avocado Oil
¼ cup Water
1 tsp - Garlic Salt
1 tsp - Onion Powder
1 tbsp – Sugar

Greek Cucumber Salad Variation:
¼ cup Fresh Dill, chopped
1 tbsp - Lemon Juice

Asian Sweet & Spicy Cucumber Salad Variation:
1 cup - Carrots, matchsticks
1 cup - Daikon Radish, matchsticks
1 tsp - Fish Sauce
1 tsp - Soy Sauce
1 tsp - Fresh Ginger, grated
1 tsp - Red Pepper Flakes

Italian Tomato & Cucumber Salad Variation:
1 cup - Grape Tomatoes, halved
1 tsp each: Basil, Fennel Seed, Oregano

1:
Prepare all ingredients
2:
Peel cucumbers then cut lengthwise. Use a spoon to remove the seeds. Then cut in ½-inch pieces.
3:
Combine all vinaigrette ingredients (plus any additions). In a large bowl, combine remaining ingredients and coat well with vinaigrette. Cover and place in refrigerator until ready to serve (at least 30 minutes but no more than 2 days).

GARLIC NOODLES

Serves: 4-6   Prep Time: 5 min   Cook Time: 25 min

1lb – Spaghetti Noodles
3 – Garlic Cloves, minced
¼ cup – Coco Aminos or Soy Sauce
1 tsp – Fish Sauce
1 tsp – Oyster Sauce
1 tsp – Ginger Powder
3 – Scallions, sliced
1 tsp – Toasted White Sesame Seeds
1 tbsp – Avocado Oil

1:
Prepare all of the ingredients. Start water boiling for pasta.
2:
In a small bowl, combine garlic, coco aminos, fish sauce, oyster sauce and ginger powder for noodles.
3:
Place pasta in boiling water and cook as directed on package. Drain in colander and rinse with cool water to arrest cooking process.
4:
In a large sauté pan or wok over medium-high heat, add oil for noodles. Add the noodles to the oil and stir to coat with oil. Stir in noodle sauce and continue to cook for 5 minutes will stirring frequently with thongs. Add green onions and sesame seeds and cook 1 minute longer.

ROASTED POTATOES & CAULIFLOWER

Serves: 4-6   Prep time: 5 min   Cook Time: 40 min

1 ½ lb – Baby Red Potatoes, quartered
1 – Cauliflower Head, cut into flowerets
1 tbsp – Avocado Oil
1 tsp each: Salt, Smoked Paprika, Dill

1:
Prepare all of the ingredients. Preheat oven to 400deg.
2:
On a large baking sheet, mix all ingredients for the potatoes and cauliflower, until evenly coated. Put in oven for 40 minutes.

STREET CORN

Serves: 4-6   Prep Time: 5 Min   Cook Time: 30 min

4-6 – Corn Ears, in husk
½ cup - Butter
½ cup – Parmesan Cheese, grated
1 tbsp – Parsley
2 tsp each: Salt, Smoked Paprika

1:
Prepare all of the ingredients. Preheat Grill or Oven to 400deg.
2:
Place corn, in husk, on grill or in oven to cook for 25 minutes. On a plate (large enough for an ear of corn) combine parmesan cheese, and seasonings. Remove corn from grill/oven at the end of cook time and allow to cool at least 5 minutes.
3:
Melt butter in a small dish. Remove husks and silks from corn. Brush with melted butter then roll in cheese mixture.

BAKED CAULIFLOWER

Serves: 4-6   Prep Time: 5 min   Cook Time: 30 min

2 – Cauliflower Heads, cut into flowerets
1 tbsp – Avocado Oil
1 tsp each: Dill, Salt, Garlic Powder

1:
Prepare all of the ingredients. Preheat oven to 425deg
2:
On a baking sheet, mix together all ingredients for cauliflower and flatten to single layer. Place on top rack of oven and bake for 30 minutes.

Variations: For spicy Cauliflower add 1 tsp Cayenne. For Curried Cauliflower replace all seasonings with curry powder. Or replace one head of cauliflower with broccoli.

SALSA

Serves: 4-6   Prep Time: 10min

Basic Salsa
1 cup Red Onion, chopped
2 cup - Roma Tomatoes, chopped
1 tsp each: Salt, Pepper
½ - Jalapeno, diced
½ cup – Cilantro, chopped
2 – Garlic Cloves, minced
2 tbsp each: Avocado Oil, Apple Cider Vinegar
1 tbsp each: Lime Juice, Sugar

Restaurant-Style Salsa Variation:
½ cup - Cilantro, chopped
1 tsp each: Cumin, Chili Powder

Corn Salsa Variation:
1 15oz can - Sweet Corn
1 tsp each: Paprika, Cumin

Mango Salsa Variation:
Omit 1 cup Tomato
1 cup - Fresh Mango, peeled and cubed
Omit Garlic

Thai Salsa Variation:
½ cup - Cilantro, chopped
½ cup Carrots, matchsticks
½ cup Red Cabbage, shredded
1 tbsp - Fresh Ginger, grated
1 tsp each: Red Pepper Flakes, Soy Sauce, Fish Sauce

Sweet Pepper Salsa
1 cup - Sweet Peppers (all colors), chopped
Omit Jalapeno Pepper

1:
Prepare all of the ingredients.
2:
Combine all ingredient for Basic Salsa. Add additional ingredients
for variation.
3:
If a more sauce like salsa is desired, use an immersion blender to
smooth out.

BUTTERED RICE

Serves: 4-6   Prep Time: 5 min   Cook Time: 20 min

2 cups – Long Grain Rice
1 qt – Chicken Broth
3 tbsp – Butter
1 tsp each: Parsley, Garlic Powder

1:
Prepare all of the ingredients
2:
In a medium pan over medium heat, add all ingredients and stir together. Cover with lid and let cook for 15 minutes. When done remove from heat and leave lid on until ready to serve.

POTATO SALAD

Serves: 4-6   Prep Time: 10 min   Cook Time: 20 min

2 lb – Baby Potatoes, halved
1 lb – Bacon, cut in ½-inch pieces
4 – Scallions, sliced
3 – Garlic Cloves, minced
5 – Celery Stalks, diced
3 – Eggs, hard-boiled, peeled, diced
12 oz – Greek Yogurt
2 tbsp – Lemon Juice
1 tsp each: Salt, Pepper, Parsley, Paprika

1:
Prepare all of the ingredients. Start water boiling for potatoes
2:
In a frying pan over medium-high heat, add bacon pieces. Cook until crispy and remove to paper towel covered plate.
3:
Add potatoes to boiling water and cook for 15 minutes. Drain and let cool for at least 5 minutes before combining.
4:
In a small bowl, combine yogurt, lemon juice and seasonings.
5:
In a large bowl, combine potatoes, garlic, celery, scallions, eggs, bacon, and yogurt mixture. Chill for at least 15 minutes before serving.

PASTA SALAD

Serves: 4-6   Prep Time: 10 min   Cook Time: 15 min

1 ½ lb – Short Pasta (Rotini, Medium Shells, Cellentani)
½ lb – Bacon, cut in ½-inch pieces
½ - Red Onion, diced
1 cup – Sweet Bell Peppers, diced
½ cup – Parmesan Cheese, shredded

For Dressing:
½ cup – Avocado Oil
1/3 cup – Apple Cider Vinegar
2 tbsp – Lemon Juice
2 tbsp – Honey
1 tsp each: Salt, Pepper, Basil, Oregano, Parsley, Garlic Powder

1:
Prepare all of the ingredients. Start water boiling for pasta.
2:
In a small bowl, combine ingredients for dressing and refrigerate.
3:
Add pasta to boiling water and cook as directed on package. Drain
in colander and rinse with cool water to arrest cooking process.
Set aside to continue to cool.
4:
In a frying pan over medium-high heat, add bacon pieces. Cook
until crispy and remove to paper towel covered plate to drain
excess grease.
5:
In a large bowl, combine pasta, bacon, onion, peppers, cheese, and
dressing. Chill for at least 15 minutes before serving

HONEY ROASTED CARROTS

Serves: 4-6   Prep Time: 10 min   Cook Time: 20 min

1 lb – Whole Carrots, peeled, cut in half lengthwise, then in 3-inch pieces
3 tbsp – Honey
1 tbsp – Avocado Oil
1 tsp each: Salt, Pepper, Parsley, Paprika

1:
Prepare all of the ingredients. Preheat oven to 400deg.
2:
In a small bowl, combine all ingredients except carrots. On a baking sheet, arrange carrot pieces in a single layer. Brush with honey mixture, turning carrots to coat evenly. Place in oven and cook for 20 minutes

PASTA IN RED SAUCE

Serves: 4-6   Prep Time: 10 min   Cook time: 15 min

1 lb – Pasta (long or short)
1 28oz can – Crushed Tomatoes
1 15oz can – Tomato Puree
½ - Red Onion, diced
3 - Garlic Cloves, minced
1 tbsp – Avocado Oil
1 tsp each: Salt, Pepper, Basil, Oregano, Red Pepper Flakes,
Fennel Seed

1:
Prepare all of the ingredients. Start water boiling for pasta.
2:
In a saucepan over medium-high heat, add oil, onions, and garlic.
Let cook 3 minutes then add crushed tomatoes, tomato puree
and seasonings. Reduce heat to medium and let simmer for 10
minutes.
3:
Add pasta to water and cook as directed on the package. Drain in
colander then rinse with cool water to arrest the cooking process.

Plating Notes: Two options – place a portion of pasta on plate and
ladle sauce over or return pasta to pan and pour sauce over to
combine before serving.

RICE & BEANS

Serves: 4-6   Prep Time: 5 min   Cook time: 20 min

For Beans:
2 15oz cans – Refried Beans
½ cup – Milk
½ cup – Sharp Cheddar Cheese, shredded
1 tsp each: Cumin, Chili Powder
For Rice:
2 cups – Long Grain Rice
1 qt – Chicken Broth
1 15oz can – Tomato Puree
2 – Garlic Cloves, minced
1 tbsp – Avocado Oil

1:
Prepare all of the ingredients.

2:
In a pot over medium-high heat, add the avocado oil for rice, and garlic. Cook for 2 minutes then add rice and cook for 5 minutes, stirring frequently. Reduce heat to medium, add broth and tomato puree, mix well. Cover and let cook for 15 minutes. Remove from heat and leave lid on until ready to serve.

3:
In a saucepan over medium heat, add refried beans, milk, and bean seasoning. Cook for 4 minutes, stirring occasionally to combine. Add cheese and mix thoroughly. Reduce heat to low and stir occasionally. Let simmer.

INDEX

Alphabetically

By Protein

COMING SOON!

Looking for more ways to have a great Burger Night with your family? Try this mouthwatering collection of over 60 burger recipes using different types of meats, cheese, and homemade toppings to shake things up. Burgers on a Weeknight is the second cookbook collection offered by Estelle Forrest (author of Homemade on a Weeknight: A Family Cookbook). With recipes for homemade BBQ Sauce, Hummus, Chili, Beer Cheese, and Herbed Yogurt (just to name a few!) you are going to flip for the variety of burger creations in this cookbook. Burgers don't have to be for summertime anymore!

Available on Amazon.com in Print of Kindle Versions!

Made in United States
Troutdale, OR
08/27/2024

22324987R00086